D0594411

Questions Christians Ask The Rabbi

Questions Christians Ask The Rabbi

Rabbi Ronald H. Isaacs

KTAV Publishing House

Library of Congress Cataloging-in-Publication Data

Isaacs, Ronald H.
  Questions Christians ask the rabbi / by Ron Isaacs.
      p. cm.
  ISBN 0-88125-924-1
  1. Judaism--Miscellanea. 2. Judaism--Essence, genius, nature. 3. Judaism--
Customs and practices. 4. Judaism--Doctrines. 5. Christianity and other
religions--Judaism. 6. Judaism--Relations--Christianity. I. Title.
BM51.I83 2006
296--dc22   2006005513

Manufactured in the United States of America

Published by
KTAV Publishing House, Inc.
930 Newark Avenue
Jersey City, NJ 07306
(201) 963-9524
FAX (201) 963-0102
www.ktav.com
Email: bernie@ktav.com

✹ Contents

The Bible   42

❋ Introduction

A few years ago, my son-in-law Aryeh Lebeau surprised me by designing a Web site, www.rabbi.ron.com. The Web site features the books I have written and allows people from across the country and in Canada to submit questions to me on subjects of Jewish interest. Much to my surprise, a good many questions came from people of the Christian faith. I was so intrigued that I began to compile a list of their questions (and my answers) in the hope that one day I would write a book in which I could share my answers with all of my readers. Bernie Scharfstein at Ktav expressed an interest in this project, and I want to thank him for his friendship and confidence in my work.

Questions Christians Ask The Rabbi is the book of my answers to the many questions I have received from Christians over these past few years. In order to make for easier reading, I have categorized the questions by topic: Jesus, the Synagogue, Jewish Beliefs, the Bible, Holidays, Life Cycle, Dietary Laws, Jews and the Community, Medical Ethics, Jews and Christians, Denominations, and Israel.

Asking questions is what Judaism is all about. I want to thank everyone who has visited my Web site for allowing me the opportunity to share my answers to your many questions. Enjoy the book, and I look forward to your continuing to send me challenging and thoughtful questions. It is always a pleasure to be in touch with you.

Rabbi Ron Isaacs

✳ Jesus

1. Do Jews really believe that Jesus lived and came to earth?

Yes, most Jewish people believe that Jesus lived, but not that he "came to earth." He did not need to travel to earth from some heavenly abode, because he was born of Jewish parents, Mary and Joseph, in about the year 4 B.C.E. It appears that he also had a number of brothers and sisters, and the Gospels mention the names of Joseph, Simon, James, and Judas. His childhood centered around the Galilee, where many of the poorer Jews resided.

The Gospel of Luke reports that when Jesus was twelve, he surprised the sages at the Temple in Jerusalem with his vast knowledge. Beyond, this, the details of his first thirty years are practically unreported.

Indeed, there is no Jewish consensus on how Jews are to regard Jesus. In recent decades many scholars have tended to view him as one of several first-and second-century Jews who claimed to be the Messiah and attempted to rid Judea of its Roman oppressors. However, almost no scholars believe that Jesus intended to start a new religion. Were Jesus to return to earth today, most Jews believe he would undoubtedly feel more at home in a synagogue than a church. An increasing number of scholars believe that Christianity's real founder was another first-century Jew, Paul.

1

2. **Do Jews believe that Jesus was Jewish?**

Yes, they do! Jesus was born of Jewish parents, Mary and Joseph. The New Testament depiction of Jesus suggests that he was a law-abiding and highly nationalistic Jew and a man with a strong sense of ethics. Like many of the ancient rabbis, he saw the love of one's neighbor as a central demand of the Jewish religion. Though many Christians are under the impression that he opposed Judaism's emphasis on law, in actuality he strongly criticized those who advocated dropping it. "Do not imagine that I have come to abolish the Law [i.e., the Torah] or the Prophets," he said to his early disciples. "I tell you solemnly, till heaven and earth disappear, not one dot, not one little stroke, shall disappear from the Law until its purpose is achieved." Jesus finished his warning by saying, "Therefore, the man who infringes even the least of these commandments and teaches others to do the same will be considered the least in the kingdom of heaven" (Matthew 5:17–19).

3. **Do Jesus's sayings in the New Testament at all conform to Jewish teachings?**

Yes, most statements attributed to Jesus in the New Testament do conform to Jewish teachings, since Jesus generally practiced Pharisaic (rabbinic) Judaism. However, there are some notable exceptions. For example, in Matthew 9:6 we are told that "the Son of Man" (Jesus) forgives all sins. Judaism believes that only God can forgive sins committed against Him. In addition, whereas Judaism believes that anyone can come to God, Jesus claimed that people could come to God only through him ("No one knows the Father [God] except the Son [Jesus], and anyone to whom the Son chooses to reveal Him" (Matthew

11:27). Finally, Jesus's attitude toward evil people is antithetical to Jewish thought. In Matthew 5:44 he says: "Love your enemies and pray for your persecutors." The Torah commands that one should offer powerful resistance to the evil person: "You shall burn the evil out from your midst" (Deuteronomy 17:7).

4. Why did Jesus eat a Passover meal and use unleavened bread?

Shortly before Passover, Jesus made his way to Jerusalem. The city was filled with thousands of Jewish pilgrims who had come to take part in the Passover observances at the Temple. Jesus himself went to the Temple and created a disturbance there by driving away the men who changed the people's money into the proper currency for the purchase of birds for sacrifices. His mission ended in failure, for by failing to denounce the Romans he antagonized the people. They expected a Messiah who would put an end to the injustices of Roman rule, while Jesus insisted that they should submit to Roman authority and pay their taxes. Discouraged and disheartened, Jesus retired with his disciples to participate in the Seder, the Passover evening meal. This meal is what has come to be known as the "Last Supper," for Roman soldiers arrested Jesus shortly thereafter while his disciples fled in panic. Jesus was later brought to Pontius Pilate, the Roman governor, who heard the charges against him and condemned him to death as a revolutionary, self-styled "king of the Jews."

5. Why was Jesus circumcised?

In line with Jewish tradition, Jesus's parents took their child to the Temple for circumcision. According to Genesis 17:11, circumcision is a sign of the covenant between God and the children of Israel. At the end of the circumcision, a Jewish child is officially given his Hebrew name. The name "Jesus" was given to the son of Mary as ordered by the angel before his birth (Luke 2:21).

Interestingly, in the early Church, one of the first arguments arose out of the fact that St. Peter insisted that males who wished to become Christians must first be circumcised, as were Jesus and every other faithful Jew. On the other hand, St. Paul preached that all a convert to Christianity needed was a "circumcision of the heart" (Romans 2:29). After a meeting of the Church leaders in Jerusalem (called the Council of Jerusalem), Paul's view prevailed, and circumcision was dropped as a requirement for Christians.

6. **Can a Jew believe in Jesus and still be Jewish?**

Judaism cannot be detached from beliefs about God. Although the major Jewish denominations affirm the critical importance of belief in an incorporeal God, they do not specify all the particulars of that belief. However, belief in a trinitarian God or in Jesus as the Son of God can never be consistent with Jewish tradition.

To Christians, Jesus is the Son of God and the Messiah. Jesus broke with a long and clearly established biblical tradition that no human being could ever be divine. Since the legal definition of a Jew is one who is born of a Jewish mother, a Jew who believes in Jesus would still technically qualify as being Jewish. However, the Jewish community would consider such a person an apostate.

7. **Who are the Jews for Jesus?**

Jews for Jesus is a Christian missionary group whose volunteers attempt to persuade Jews to accept the notion that one can remain a Jew and believe in Jesus. This group is the best-known and most public of the missionizers. Jews for Jesus was founded in 1973 by the Reverend Martin (Moishe) Rosen, a Jew who underwent conversion and was ordained a Baptist minister in 1956. It currently spends millions of dollars annually for aggressive advertising, newspaper ads, and activities in transportation centers and college campuses.

Several years ago a member of my own temple was out of town and went to what he thought was a synagogue service on Friday evening (the Jewish Sabbath). He knew something seemed strange, but was not exactly sure. There was no cross or any other traditional Christian symbol. The name of Jesus was not mentioned, but the Hebrew equivalent, Yeshua, was. The congregational leader called himself a rabbi. Sabbath candles were lit, and the Kiddush blessing over the wine was recited. Later, my congregant learned that he had attended a Jews for Jesus temple.

8. **Who were the Pharisees, and why did Jesus call them hypocrites?**

"Woe to you, scribes and Pharisees, hypocrites, for you are like whitewashed tombs, which outwardly appear beautiful, but within they are of dead men's bones" (Matthew 23:27). These poignant words, uttered by Jesus, were levied against a popular Jewish sect of his day known as the Pharisees. At the time this group numbered some 600 people. The Pharisees' understanding of Judaism was characterized by their belief in the Oral Law. They believed that when God gave the Torah (the first five books of the Bible) to Moses, God also gave him an oral tradition that specified precisely how the laws in the Torah were to be carried out. For example, although the Torah demands "an eye for an eye," the Pharisees maintained that God never intended that physical retribution was to be exacted. Rather, a person who blinded another was required to pay monetary compensation for his loss. The Pharisees also believed that the Oral Law empowered them to introduce necessary changes into Jewish law, and to apply the law to unanticipated circumstances.

The Pharisees were the ancestors of contemporary Judaism. The other sects that existed contemporaneously with them died out shortly after the destruction of the Second Temple. Once they disappeared, the Pharisees were no longer called by that name. Unfortunately, at the very time all Jews were increasingly identifying as Pharisees, the word began to acquire a new, highly pejorative meaning. The New Testament repeatedly depicted them as religious hypocrites. Eventually, the word "pharisee" itself came to be synonymous in English with "hypocrite."

Jesus felt that many Pharisees were interested only in the outward signs of righteousness and had forgotten that genuine religion is that which comes from the heart. He felt that Pharisees were so intent on keeping the letter of the law that they missed the more important dimensions of faith and life. Once, for example, when Jesus healed a man with a withered hand on the holy Sabbath, some Pharisees questioned whether it was proper for him to do so, since no work was to be performed on the seventh day (Matthew 23:23). Jesus responded to their challenge by asking: "What man of you, if he has one sheep and it falls into a pit on the Sabbath, will not lay hold of it and lift it out? Of how much more value is man than a sheep. So it is lawful to do good on the Sabbath" (Matthew 23:23).

It is the ultimate irony that a Pharisee named Saul of Tarsus, who eventually joined the followers of Jesus, became an influential leader of the early Church, and authored what many regard as the finest treatise on love in the New Testament (I Corinthians 13). Saul was later known as St. Paul!

9. **Is it true that Jesus got the idea of teaching in parables from the Jews?**

Yes, Jesus taught his disciples and other interested listeners through parables, a familiar educational method in his day. Parables were stories (whether true or fictitious) that revealed moral truths. Teaching by using parables is very much a part of the Jewish tradition. The Hebrew Bible, known as the Tanach, records a number of famous parables. Perhaps the most famous is related to King David. When the prophet Nathan confronted David with the word of God's judgment for his murder of Uriah in order to steal Uriah's wife (Bathsheba), Nathan brought the king to repentance by telling the parable of the rich man's sheep and the poor man's beloved lamb (II Samuel 12:1–4).

10. **Do Jews believe that Jesus was able to perform so many miracles as recorded in the New Testament?**

There is no biblical Hebrew word for "miracle." The closest related words are "wonder" (*mofet*) and "sign" (*ot*). Our ancestors regarded the miracles of the Bible as literally true and authentic. They did not differentiate between the natural and the supernatural, since it was the one omnipotent God who caused all to be and set the course of nature according to His will. Thus the dividing of the Red Sea and the manna from heaven were accepted as standard historical events, with the Bible itself making no reference to the miraculous nature of these happenings. In God's world, there is nothing that is impossible.

In contradistinction to Judaism's somewhat reserved attitude toward miracles and its rejection of them as affirmations of religious truths, miracles play a very important role in Christianity. The Gospels are one long record of miracles performed by Jesus. While Judaism refuses to

acknowledge miracles as proof of divine authorization, the
Gospels adduce the miraculous acts of Jesus as proof.
Each miracle performed by Jesus was designed to reveal
that he held the power of God to perform such works, illus-
trating not only divine authorization, but his own divinity.

Since traditional Jews rarely would be seen reading the
New Testament (unless they were studying it in some com-
parative religion course), it is likely that most of them
would have no opinion as to whether Jesus's so-called miracles were factualy.

11. **Who do Jews believe killed Jesus?**

The Roman governor Pontius Pilate was the execution-
er of Jesus. As portrayed in the New Testament he was
gentle and kind-hearted, but many scholars regard this as
fictional. Like most fictions, the story was created with a
purpose. When the New Testament was written,
Christianity was banned by Roman law. The Romans, well
aware that they had executed Christianity's founder, had
no reason to rescind their anti-Christian legislation.
Christianity's only hope for gaining true legitimacy was to
prove to Rome that the crucifixion had been a terrible
error, and had only come about because the Jews had
forced Pilate to do it. Thus, the New Testament depicts
Pilate as wishing to spare Jesus from punishment. This
account ignores one simple fact. Pilate's power in Judea
was absolute. Had he really wanted to absolve Jesus, he
could have done so. He certainly would not have allowed a
mob of Jews, whom he detested, to force him to kill someone he admired.

Crucifixion, a Roman form of execution, was forbidden
by Jewish law because it was torture. Some 50,000 to
100,000 Jews were themselves crucified by the Romans in
the first century. How ironic, therefore, that Jews have his-

torically been associated with the cross as the ones who brought about Jesus's crucifixion.

12. **Why don't Jews accept Jesus as the Messiah?**

From the Jewish standpoint, history is still in the making and fulfillment is yet to be achieved: the Messiah will come "in the end of days," when the purpose or goal of history is fulfilled. In Christianity, the Messiah has already come, and the purpose of history has been fulfilled in him.

The Jewish Messiah is a mortal man, albeit a great personality endowed with remarkable spiritual and mental qualities, appointed by God to carry out an appointed task. He is human. Therefore in Judaism, because of the claim that he was the Son of God, Jesus must be disqualified as the Messiah.

The Jewish Messiah is an instrument of God. Only God is our Rock and our Redeemer. In Christianity, Jesus himself is both Savior and Redeemer.

The Jewish Messiah, by definition, must be of the seed of David. The suggestion that the Messiah will be the son of God is completely alien to Jewish thinking. The Christian Messiah (Jesus) is considered to be the son of God, born of a human mother by an immaculate conception.

Finally, the Jewish Messiah is an instrument for bringing divine redemption to society. The Christian Messiah brings redemption to the individual soul.

13. **Did the prophets actually predict the coming of Jesus as the Messiah?**

Some Christians think so, though today most Christian and Jewish scholars would agree that none of the prophets, writing 750 years before Jesus was born, had him or anyone like him in mind when they wrote.

Christians who seek to establish this claim most commonly cite references to the so-called "servant passages" from the writings of Isaiah. In at least three passages the "servant" is described in the Hebrew Bible as a male individual chosen by God to do God's bidding:

> This is My servant, whom I uphold,
> My chosen one, in whom I delight
> I put My spirit upon him,
> He shall teach the true way to the nations.
>
> (Isaiah 42:1–2)

Throughout the ages, Christians have read, sung, and taught this and other passages to justify their belief that Jesus's birth, life, and death were all telegraphed by Judaism. Since they believe that this is the case, many Christians wonder how it is possible for Jews not to accept Jesus as the Messiah.

The first thing to observe is that in the writings of Isaiah, the servant is identified as "the people of Israel," not as an individual. God speaks:

> But you, Israel, My servant,
> Jacob, who, I have chosen.
>
> (Isaiah 41:8)

Isaiah wanted the people of Israel to understand that they had an active role to play in redeeming the world. It is not God's work alone. Today, most biblical scholars agree that the servant about whom Isaiah wrote was not an individual, certainly not one who was to be born six centuries later, but the Jewish people who lived then, in the prophet's day, and who had a special mission to perform.

14. **Was Jesus a prophet?**

While some Christians think Jesus was a prophet in the great tradition of literary prophecy, Jews do not. Jesus lived 500 years after the death of the prophet Malachi (516 B.C.E.), the last of the literary prophets. Jesus may have rejected the designation of prophet for himself, preferring instead to let some think of him as divine. The New Testament suggests this:

Now when Jesus came into the district of Caesarea Philippi, he asked his disciples, "Who do men say the Son of man is?" And they said, "Some say John the Baptist, others say Elijah, and others Jeremiah or one of the prophets."

He said to them, " But who do you say that I am?" Simon Peter replied, "You are the Christ, the Son of the living God." And Jesus answered him, "Blessed are you, Simon Bar Jonah! For flesh and blood has not revealed this to you, but My father who is in heaven."

(Matthew 16:13–17)

No prophet ever made such a claim or permitted others so to think of him. In doing so, Jesus broke with a long-established biblical tradition that no human being could ever be divine.

Jesus's death was more important than his life. The Israelite prophets viewed their task as helping people to free themselves from the oppression of stronger nations. Jesus saw his life as one which, through his death, would redeem all people from sin. His followers, and those who later wrote about him, portrayed Jesus as believing that he was born for the express purpose of dying in order to redeem mankind.

15. **Why do Jews often choose not to refer to Jesus as Christ?**

The term "Christ" is the English form of the Greek word *Christos*, meaning "the anointed one." Just as kings in the Bible were anointed upon taking office, so Christians consider Jesus as the anointed King of kings and Lord of lords (Revelation 19:16). In other words, the full meaning behind the Greek term is "Messiah." Because Jews do not believe in Jesus as the Messiah, they would typically refrain from referring to him as Jesus Christ.

16. **Who were the Sadducees and why did Jesus pose a threat to them?**

Jesus's popularity with the people in Jerusalem disturbed the Sadducees, another religious sect of his day. The Sadducees, rivals of the Pharisees, were aristocratic and very wealthy. They had a vested interest in maintaining the status quo in both religion and the government. They did not want anyone to "rock the boat," so to speak. Therefore, when the people flocked to hear Jesus and responded so zealously to his preaching that some wanted to make him a king (John 6:15), he posed a threat to the current religious and political scene. The concern of the Sadducees was heightened all the more when the people referred to Jesus as "King of the Jews."

17. **Is there much written about Jesus in traditional Jewish texts?**

There is little written about Jesus, especially in the Talmud. Jesus appeared at a time of turmoil in Jewish history, when Herod and the Roman procurators occupied center stage in Jewish history. Jesus and his small group of followers were relatively insignificant. By the time the Talmud (the rabbinic interpretation of the Bible) was written down in its final form some 500 years after the death of Jesus, little or no information about him was available. Consequently, few references to Jesus appear in the early editions of the Talmud, and in the year 1580 the Church forced Jews to expunge all references to Jesus from future editions.

18. **Why are some fundamentalist Christians so very supportive of Israel?**

Many Christian fundamentalists travel to Israel each year, and in large numbers. Essentially, as I understand it, evangelical Christians are dedicated to the goal of converting Jews to Christianity. They have several reasons for doing this. Jesus was a Jew and Christians claim he was the Messiah; the messianic idea posited that a man at the end of days would usher in an era of world peace. The Jewish lack of acceptance of Jesus has always been a disturbing phenomenon for the Church. For evangelical Christians, the conversion of the Jews is directly linked to the credibility of the cross and the second coming of the Messiah.

Fundamentalist Christians are also consumed with the Apocalypse and what will happen at the end of days. The Bible sees this as the time when nations will attack Israel over the status of Jerusalem. But the view of messianic days in Matthew 23:39 is where Jesus declares "I will not return until you [the Jews] say 'blessed be He who comes in the name of the Lord.' " This is interpreted by the Church to mean that Jesus cannot come again to bring a truly messianic era on earth until all the Jews have been converted, including the several million currently living in Israel.

19. For what audience was the Book of Matthew written?

The Book of Matthew was written primarily for a Jewish audience. The book clearly shows that Jesus was the Jewish Messiah, a king, and that he was descended from David and Abraham. Matthew records the story of the wise men visiting the baby Jesus, an event fitting for a king. Luke records the humbler story of the shepherds visiting Jesus.

20. What day is Jesus's birthday?

December 25 was celebrated as the birth date of Jesus by the early fourth century C.E., and probably much earlier. This date was probably selected because the Romans celebrated the Mithraic festival of the sun god on that day, and this was an opportunity to make a pagan festival into a religious one. This date was also near the winter solstice. The Eastern Church celebrates Christmas on January 6. The exact date of Jesus's birth is unknown, although biblical historians place it some time around the year 6 before the common era.

21. What was the Hebrew name of Jesus?

The name Jesus is related to the Hebrew names Joshua and Isaiah, which mean "one who saves" or "God saves." His name in Hebrew may have been Yashu, from the word for "salvation." The angel told Jesus's mother, Mary, to call him Jesus because he would save his people from their sins (Matthew 1:21).

22. **Did Jesus have siblings?**

The New Testament mentions Jesus's brothers a number of times and his sister twice. In two passages, several brothers are mentioned, along with his sisters: "Is not this the carpenter's son? Is not his mother called Mary? Are not his brothers James and Joseph and Simon and Judas? Are not all his sisters with us?" (Matthew 13:55–56). They are also mentioned in Mark 6:3.

Several theories explain the nature of Jesus's brothers. One holds that they were step-brothers, Joseph's children by another marriage. A second theory holds that they were actually his cousins. A third holds that they were true blood brothers (half-brothers). The first two views preserve a doctrine of the perpetual virginity of Mary, held in the Roman Catholic and Orthodox wings of the Church, and the third (held by the Protestants) does not.

23. **Who were the Zealots?**

A small minority of Jews in Jesus's day were Zealots—Jewish revolutionaries. They were radical patriots and chafed under pagan Roman rule. They constantly agitated against the Romans and were responsible for the revolts that led to the destruction of Jerusalem in 70 C.E. One of Jesus's disciples, Simon the Zealot, had been a member.

24. **Who were the Essenes?**

The Essenes were an ascetic group of Jews in the time of Jesus who rigorously observed the Sabbath and other biblical laws. They worked at agriculture and other pursuits, remained celibate, cared for their elderly, and owned all things in common. Many have suggested that the Jews

living by the Dead Sea, at Qumran (where the Dead Sea
Scrolls were discovered), were an Essene community.

25. **What is an apostle?**

The word "apostle" comes from the Greek word *aposto-
los*, meaning "to send." In secular Greek usage, it often
meant a ship or a naval expedition, but almost never did it
mean a person who was being sent for a purpose. In the
New Testament, the meaning was attached to people
appointed (or sent) to special functions in the church.
Usually it referred to the twelve disciples of Jesus or to
Paul.

26. **Where did Jesus die and where was he buried?**

Jesus died at a place called Golgotha, which is Aramaic
for "skull," but its exact location is disputed. Scholars
today believe that the Church of the Holy Sepulcher marks
the true site of Golgotha. Jesus was buried in a rock-cut
tomb sealed with a large stone. The Garden Tomb near
Gordon's Calvary is thought by some to be the site of
Jesus's burial, but it is possible the tomb is somewhere
under the present-day Church of the Holy Sepulcher
The Chapel of the Ascension on the Mount of Olives
supposedly marks the spot where Jesus ascended to heav-
en. It was built during Crusader times in the eleventh century, over a spot marked since the fourth century. A stone
slab contains what some claim are Jesus's last footprints
on earth.

27. **How long was Jesus dead?**

The total time that Jesus was dead was not much more
than thirty-six hours. According to the Gospels, Jesus died

on Friday afternoon, about 3:00 p.m. He was placed in a tomb that evening and remained there until sometime early Sunday morning, before the women got there. The popular notion of three days comes from the Jewish way of counting days, in which any portion of a day counts as a full day.

❀ The Synagogue

1. Are there any fixed rules for synagogue architecture?

There are no stylistic guidelines for synagogue architecture. Synagogues have diverse forms and styles throughout the world. Nevertheless, there are some features common to nearly all synagogues.

The most fundamental components of the congregational prayer service are said while facing Jerusalem. Since Jerusalem lies due east from America, the front of most American synagogue interiors will be the eastern wall. Traditionally, a synagogue must have at least one window facing east toward Jerusalem. Windows are a way of ensuring that people can see the outside, thus making their prayers more inclusive.

2. What exactly is the Holy Ark, and what is inside it?

At the front of the synagogue (on the east wall) is the Holy Ark (*aron ha-kodesh* in Hebrew). Like the original Ark, this is a cabinet in which the Torah scrolls (i.e,. the Five Books of Moses handwritten in Hebrew on a parchment scroll) are housed. The scrolls will be hidden behind a cur-

tain or doors, or both. This is reminiscent of the arrange-
ment in the Temple, where the Ark containing the pact
between Jews and God was kept behind a curtain in the
Holy of Holies.

It is the presence of the Torah scrolls within the Ark
that gives the synagogue its measure of holiness and sanctity.

3. **What is the purpose of the light above the Holy Ark?**

Suspended above the Holy Ark is the *ner tamid*, the so-
called Eternal Light. It has no liturgical function. In the
ancient Temple, the Eternal Light was the westernmost
light of the seven-branched candelabrum, called the menorah. It is a reminder of the Divine Presence and the eternal
faith of the Jewish people

4. **What is the symbolism of the seven-branched can-
delabrum?**

The seven-branched candelabrum is called a menorah.
The original menorah had an important function in the
ancient Temple. It was provided each day with fresh olive
oil, and burned from morning to evening. The menorah
symbolizes the creation of the universe in seven days—the
center light represents the Sabbath. The seven branches
are also said to allude to the continents of the earth as well
as the seven heavens, guided by the light of God.
Frequently used as a symbol of Judaism and the Jewish
people, a representation of the menorah has been found on
tombs and monuments dating from the first century. The
earliest-preserved and most authentic representation of
the Temple menorah is depicted on the arch of Titus commemorating the triumphal parade following the destruction of Jerusalem in the year 70.

5. **Why do women have their own separate seating area in traditional synagogues?**

In Orthodox synagogues, women have their own spe-cial section where they are seated. This area is reminiscent of the special women's section in the ancient Temple in Jerusalem. The purpose of the special area for women is to separate them from the men. The ancient rabbis felt that there would be less distraction if men and women did not sit together while worshiping.

6. **What are the roles of the rabbi and the cantor in the synagogue?**

The word "rabbi" means teacher. Accordingly, the rabbi gives sermons, explains the service, often announces the pages, and recites blessings during services. Aside from these functions in the synagogue service, the rabbi also acts as teacher, counselor, and leader of the congregation.

The cantor chants and leads the congregants in prayer. The cantor in some synagogues also reads the Torah, teaches the Bar and Bat Mitzvah students, and acts as spiritual leader and counselor like the rabbi.

7. **What are the various prayer garments worn by wor-shipers during prayer services?**

Centuries ago, the Talmud (book of rabbinic law) sug-gested that to cover one's head was a sign of respect and humility before God. The *yarmulke*, or skullcap (*kippah* in Hebrew), is the preferred headgear for Jewish men who attend synagogue. Orthodox Jewish men generally keep their heads covered both outside and inside the syna-gogue. In Reform congregations, which tend to be more lib-eral, the wearing of a head covering is optional.

In biblical times, women covered their heads with veils or scarves as a sign of modesty. Today, most Orthodox women cover their hair when they appear in public both outside and inside the synagogue. In Reform and Conservative synagogues, covering the head for women is generally optional.

The *tallit*, or prayer shawl, is worn by men (and some women) as a reminder to perform *mitzvot*, religious obligations. Centuries ago, God commanded Moses to speak to the Israelites and bid them to affix fringes to the corners of their overgarments as a sign of God's commandments.

During the week at Jewish worship services one might see men (and some women in more liberal settings) wearing *tefillin*. These are small black leather boxes with straps attached to them. They are worn in conformance with the biblical command to "bind them for a sign upon your hand and for frontlets between your eyes" (Deuteronomy 6:8). Inside the boxes are parchments with sections from the Five Books of Moses. The tefillin are a sign of faith and devotion. It is the Jewish way of binding oneself to God.

8. Why do Jews pray in Hebrew?

Hebrew is the holy tongue of the Jewish people. As the language of the Torah, the Five Books of Moses, it is the preferred language. However, according to Jewish law, prayers need not be said in Hebrew, but in any language one understands. A Hasidic tale illustrates the spirit of this ruling:

A boy from a rural village where there were few Jews and no synagogue once went into town with his father to do some shopping. Finding the town synagogue, he entered it and wanted to pray. But he did not know how. His father had taught him the letters of the Hebrew alphabet, but no more than that. So a thought occurred to him. He began to recite the Hebrew alphabet over and over again. And then he said: "O God, You know what it is that I want to say. You put the letters together so they make the right words."

That too was a Jewish prayer!

9. **What is a Bar Mitzvah?**

According to Jewish law, when a boy becomes age thirteen (according to his birthday in the Hebrew calendar), he becomes responsible to perform God's obligations, called *mitzvot*. To mark this occasion of his Bar Mitzvah (becoming a "son of the commandments"), it is customary for a boy to chant a Haftarah (a selection from one of the books of the Hebrew prophets) and sometimes also to read from the Torah (the Five Books of Moses). To be able to do this requires much preparation and study. In many synagogues a girl can celebrate a Bat Mitzvah ("daughter of the commandments"). Much like a boy, she too is called to the Torah and chants a prophetic portion.

10. **Does the United States have a chief rabbi?**

No, each branch of Judaism in the United States has its ordained rabbis, but there is no chief rabbi. Each synagogue rabbi is the adjudicator in religious disputes and has the authority to make Jewish decisions for his congregation. The State of Israel does have a chief rabbi (actually two), as do some European countries.

11. **Are synagogue services open to non-Jews?**

Absolutely they are, and many rabbis encourage people of other faiths to pay visits to learn about Judaism and its customs and rituals. My own synagogue has quite a number of interfaith couples, and it is quite common for the non-Jewish partner to attend worship services, some on a fairly regular basis. Some are even able to read Hebrew and follow the service!

12. Why are representations of the Ten Commandments often used as synagogue decorations?

According to the Bible (Exodus 34), the Ten Commandments were brought down from Mount Sinai by Moses. They were placed in the ark, which accompanied the Israelites during their journey in the wilderness. It is because of this that the Ten Commandments have become a popular synagogue decorative motif, often found embroidered on the Ark curtain or on the Torah mantle.

13. What is the purpose of the silver ornamentation on the top of the Torah scrolls?

The Torah scroll is the holiest object in Jewish life. It is therefore natural to "crown" it with the symbol of kingship, and thus one often sees a silver crown adorning a Torah. *Rimmonim* are decorative crowns with little bells that fit over each of the two Torah handles. The bells were probably inspired by the vestment worn by the High Priest which also was decorated with golden bells (Exodus 28:33).

14. What differentiates a more liberal synagogue from a more traditional one?

The oldest denominational form of Judaism in America is Orthodoxy. The word "Orthodox" means "right belief," and it was applied to Jews who firmly refused to change their beliefs and observances when they came to the New World. Orthodox synagogues are most noted for women and men sitting in separate sections, in order that they do not become a distraction to each other.

The most liberal of synagogue movements is the Reform movement. Reform Judaism was born in the hope that changes would stop the wave of assimilation that was stealing thousands of Jews away from their faith. One will often hear music (typically the organ) at Sabbath services in a Reform synagogue. In many Reform synagogues the prayer shawl and wearing of a head covering are optional.

Conservative Judaism, the movement in which I serve, had its beginnings in Germany. Its motto is "tradition and change." Although men and women sit together in Conservative synagogues, much of the liturgy is in Hebrew and replicates that which would be seen in Orthodox synagogues. Men wear prayer shawls and keep their heads covered during worship services. Some women also wear prayer shawls and wear hats.

The youngest of the religious movements in American Judaism is Reconstructionism. A uniquely American movement, it began in 1922, and its leaders and thinkers are all American-born. There is more personal autonomy in the Reconstructionist movement. Typically, though, as in Conservative synagogues, men (and many women) wear prayer shawls. Head coverings are required for men, and some women wear hats as well. The liturgy is chanted predominantly in Hebrew.

15. **Why do some Jews sway when they pray in synagogue?**

The custom of swaying (called "shuckling" in the Yiddish language) while praying is an old one. There are some worshipers who sway slightly while they pray, while others do so with greatly exaggerated and rapid movement of the body. Swaying during prayer is primarily a matter of habit, and the result of early training. One explanation for the swaying custom is that it symbolizes a verse in psalms: "All my limbs shall declare, O God, who is like unto You" (Psalm 35:10). People who sway feel that it is an aid to concentration. Personally, I enjoy swaying, particularly when I am singing a lively prayer tune with the rest of the congregation. It helps my concentration and adds to my personal devotion.

16. **Why is kneeling rarely seen at prayer services?**

Bowing and kneeling were an integral part of the ceremonies and rituals in the Jerusalem Temple. In the Book of Nehemiah, we are told that after Ezra blessed God, the people bowed their heads and fell down before God with their faces to the ground. When Christianity adopted kneeling as a prayer posture, the ancient rabbis prohibited it in Jewish worship. The only exception was on Yom Kippur, the Day of Atonement, when Jews fast for twenty-four hours. During the Avodah service, when an account of the ancient Temple service is read, the cantor kneels and prostrates himself, as did the High Priest when he officiated back in Temple times. For many congregants, this is one of the highlights of the Day of Atonement service.

17. **I have seen Jewish worshipers close their eyes during prayer services. Why do they do this?**

To deepen concentration and block out distraction while reciting certain prayers, some people close their eyes and cover them with the palm of one hand. Others cover their heads with their prayer shawls to keep out all potential distraction. If you've never tried closing your eyes while praying, give it a try. You will be amazed at your increased level of concentration.

18. **Is there a reason why Jews do not include the recitation of the Ten Commandments in their prayer service?**

The Ten Commandments, one of the most significant elements in the Bible, has not been incorporated into the Jewish worship service. According to the Talmud (Berachot 12a), the Ten Commandments were recited in the ancient Jerusalem Temple as part of the daily liturgy. But the custom of reciting them was abolished to refute the claim of certain heretics who asserted that only the Ten Commandments were divinely ordained.

Today the Ten Commandments are included as an additional supplementary reading in many Jewish prayer books. They are also read on the Festival of Shavuot, which according to tradition is the time when Moses received the Ten Commandments atop of Mount Sinai.

19. **What is the difference between a synagogue and a temple?**

These two terms are largely interchangeable. Neither are Hebrew terms: "synagogue" comes from the Greek for "bringing together," and temple from the Latin word *templum*. A generation or two ago, "temple" was used to denote a modern religious institution, and "synagogue" more often referred to an Orthodox house of worship. Today, these distinctions hardly apply. My congregation where I serve as a rabbi is called Temple Sholom, and it is a Conservative synagogue.

20. **I have seen the Star of David on the Ark curtain of many synagogues. What is its significance?**

The star of David, or Magen David as it is known in Hebrew, is a six-pointed star made up of two triangles in opposite directions. Interestingly, the star has no ancient Jewish origin or religious meaning. It became a popular symbol in Jewish life about three hundred years ago in Central Europe.

Whatever its true origin, the Star of David has become a distinctively Jewish symbol. The flag of the modern State of Israel is a white banner with two horizontal blue bars, and between them the Star of David.

21. When should guests arrive when they come to prayer services, and where should they sit?

It is customary for guests who are not Jewish to arrive at the scheduled time at Reform and Reconstructionist services. For Orthodox and Conservative ones, where services tend to be longer, a non-Jewish guest may want to ask his or her host what time to arrive in order to be present for the specific event for which you have been invited. Guests may sit wherever they wish. In Orthodox synagogues, be reminded that men sit separately from women

22, Is a non-Jew expected to do anything other than sit during the worship service?

They are expected to stand when the congregation stands, out of respect for the congregation. It is optional for them to read prayers aloud and sing with congregants if this would not be a violation of their religious beliefs. They will never have to kneel, since kneeling is not a part of Jewish tradition.

23. I recently visited a synagogue that had many names on a plaque with lights next to them. What is this?

This is called a Yahrzeit plaque, and many synagogues have them in their sanctuaries. When a Jewish person dies, the custom is to light a candle in the home on the anniversary of the person's death and to pledge charity in memory of the person. The synagogue plaque has on it the name of many of the deceased members of the synagogue or their relatives. The names often appear in both English and Hebrew, and also included is the date of death in Hebrew. A small light is affixed next to each of the names, and is lit on the anniversary of the death as a way of honoring and remembering the person.

24. **Is there such a thing as a Jewish healing service?**

Healing is very much an ancient part of Jewish tradition, and many synagogues have healing services. We have one each year in our own synagogue. These healing services are eclectic and varied. There are generally common elements to most of them, including meditation, music, prayer, guided visualizations, teaching based on Jewish sources, and physical contact such as holding hands. Very often a healing service may be related to the theme of a Jewish holiday that falls at the time the healing service takes place. Music and singing are also fairly common to healing services, and a number of collections of Jewish healing music are sold through Web sites and at Judaic shops.

✳ Jewish Beliefs

1. According to Judaism, what is the meaning of life?

Being a good person is clearly at the essence of Judaism. Life is considered a gift from God, and we Jews are to make the best of this gift by doing good for ourselves and for others too. Judaism has a special system of mitzvot (divine obligations). They are all of the do's and don'ts in the Five Books of Moses. By following them diligently, one will stay on the just and righteous path.

The Book of Deuteronomy tells us "to follow God and walk in God's ways." I understand this phrase to mean that we should follow the attributes of God. For instance, just as God clothed Adam and Eve, so should we give clothing to those in need. Just as God visited Abraham when he was sick following his circumcision, so we too should make it our duty to visit sick people. All acts of justice and goodness are closely connected with the concept of honoring God's name by following God's ways.

My favorite Bible verse is from the Book of Micah 6:8. It offers wise advice to those who want to know what God really wants from us: "God has told you what is good, and what God wants of you. Do justly, love goodness, and walk humbly with your God."

2. **Do Jews believe in heaven and hell?**

The word "hell" is not part of the Jewish vocabulary. The Hebrew Bible (usually referred to by the Christian community as the Old Testament) uses the term Gehinom, which in some circles has been understood as referring to hell. In fact, Gehinom is a term borrowed from an actual place name, Gei-Ben Hinom, located south of Jerusalem. It was a valley where the wicked sacrificed their children to false gods. When Jews learned about the concept of hell from their neighbors, they often used this appropriate name to signify the home of the wicked beyond the grave.

Over time, Gehinom passed into use as a metaphoric designation for the place of punishment in the hereafter. Despite the many differences of opinion as to the true meaning of Gehinom, it is nowhere considered to be a dogma or a doctrine of faith that Jews are required to profess.

Heaven is also generally understood metaphorically as God's abode in the skies above. It does not refer to some good place to which the souls of all deceased persons will return upon their deaths. The Bible does not have a direct reference to a concrete or physical world to come, but rather some vague, poetic allusions to an afterlife. Today, it is a fundamental belief in Judaism to believe in the immortality of the soul, an immortality whose nature is known only to God. But it is not part of Jewish faith to accept any literal concept of heaven or hell. In fact, Jews have always been more concerned with this world than the next and have always concentrated their religious efforts toward building an ideal world for the living.

3. **Do Jews believe in an eye for an eye?**

Few references in the Bible are more misunderstood than the ancient Hebrew law of an eye for an eye. In Israel, for instance, it is often understood in a pejorative manner. Critics often accuse the Israeli army of practicing eye-for-an-eye morality for immediate retaliation against terrorist attacks. Centuries ago, Jewish law made detailed stipulations that an eye for an eye was to be understood as monetary compensation for injury, much as modern insurance contracts are apt to do today. An eye for an eye today is a graphic way of expressing the abstract idea that the punishment should not be too lenient or too harsh but should fit the crime and the circumstances.

4. **Do Jews believe in the devil?**

There are a number of references to Satan in the Jewish Bible. It is doubtful whether Jews ever took these references literally. In Judaism, Satan was the mythical figure of all the evil forces in the world. At times, he was identified with the Tempter—the evil impulse that prompts us to heed the worst side of human nature. But even this notion was never too deeply rooted, for Judaism teaches that God is the Creator of both good and evil, and God's dominion alone is real.

By and large, Satan in Jewish lore is most identified with the evil impulse, the lower passions that are a hindrance to our pursuit of the nobler things in life. This can serve as a useful reminder of the all-too-frequent human tendency to rationalize sinful conduct into saintly behavior, or to seek the line of least resistance in a situation that calls for tenacity and courage. Eradicating Satan from our lives can symbolize the need for us to wage war against the evil in ourselves.

5. Do Jews believe that the world was created in six days?

Yes, some Jewish traditionalists and others believe that the world was literally created by God in six days. Personally, I do not and never did. Great Jewish scholars and medieval commentators did not consider the details of the biblical account of creation theologically binding.

Evolution and scientific dating need not be considered to contradict any of the moral and spiritual views of the biblical creation story, and numbers in the Bible were rarely ever taken literally. A single day in the creation story might well symbolize several million years.

For me, the creation story is meant to teach a number of things that we cannot learn from science—for example, that God creates, that the universe is eternal, and that the universe was conceived by God's will for a reason, and is still evolving according to God's words. The sanctity of the Sabbath is also established in the creation story, as is the fact that all people are made in God's image.

6. Do Jews believe in Armageddon?

In the Book of Ezekiel, there is a prophecy of messianic days called the "War of Gog and Magog" (chap. 38), which bears a similarity to the Armageddon of the New Testament. Ezekiel foretells that the restoration of Israel to the land of its fathers will not pass unchallenged. Armies under the leadership of Gog will invade Israel, but the invasion will end in the destruction of Gog and his confederate forces. The identity of Gog is vague, and he is generally understood as an apocalyptic figure, personifying forces hostile to Israel, rather than as a particular person. Magog in the Book of Ezekiel is the country of Gog, but in rabbinic literature Magog becomes his inseparable partner, and the war of Gog and Magog appears to be the great Armageddon that will immediately precede the messianic age. Note that the names Gog and Magog are similar in sound to Armageddon.

Armageddon is not mentioned prior to the New Testament, but it is believed by some to be a corrupt spelling of Megiddo, a city mentioned numerous times in the Bible. The Book of Revelation in the New Testament refers to Armageddon as the site of the final and conclusive battle between good and evil.

7. Is Judaism a fatalistic religion?

Generally speaking, Judaism is not a fatalistic religion. Jews are masters of their own destiny, and have freedom of choice, even though most believe that God knows what the future will hold for them. Jews also believe that the severity of any divine decree can be assuaged through the giving of charity, prayer, and repenting.

8. Why are Jews called the chosen people?

The idea that Jews are the chosen people of God and have a special relationship with God stems from the Bible. Deuteronomy 7:6 describes this relationship: "For you, Israel, are a holy people unto God; God has chosen you from all the peoples on the face of the earth, to be His treasured people.

Chosenness does not mean that the Jews have been singled out for special favors. Rather, it means being selected to carry out the special duties of being God's servant. Twenty-six centuries ago, the prophet Isaiah expanded upon the idea of the Jews as the chosen ones by saying: "I have given you as a covenant to the people. For a light to the nations, to open the eyes of the blind" (Isaiah

42:6–7). This verse is very significant, for it means that according to Isaiah, the Jewish people were assigned the special mission of improving the world and teaching other peoples to see the light. So Jews understand that being chosen is not a privilege about which to boast, but rather a responsibility and a task to be undertaken. It requires contributing to the betterment of the world, which ultimately means increased responsibility.

9. **What is the Jewish view of sin?**

Various Hebrew words are used in the Five Books of Moses to denote sin. Though they are often used interchangeably, their primary signification reveals the inner meaning of the biblical conception of sin. The Hebrew word *chet*, which is used most frequently, means "missing the mark." That is to say, good action leads to a positive result, while sinful action leads to no result.

In Judaism, a person who sins is to repent and make every endeavor not to make the same mistake again.

10. **Do miracles play a big part in Jewish thought?**

Unlike Christianity, in which miracles play a large role (the Gospels are one long record of miracles performed by Jesus), Judaism has a more reserved attitude toward them. Judaism differentiates between the so-called hidden miracle and the revealing miracle. Hidden miracles are occurrences so mundane that their wondrous nature is overlooked. Judaism and its thinkers have been much more interested in the "miracles" that are evident each day: the air we breathe, the fact that the sun rises and sets, the beauty of nature's creations (flowers, plants, rivers). Life itself is considered a hidden miracle, so often taken for granted unless illness strikes.

The other type of miracle is the revealing miracle, a powerful, extraordinary event that contradicts the normal scheme of nature. This is the kind of miracle in which it is believed that God supernaturally intervenes to change the normal course of events. Although Judaism does say that God is certainly capable of performing this kind of miracle, it discourages us from wanting God to interrupt His own laws of nature. Instead, rabbinic thinkers have encouraged us to be cognizant each day of the countless miracles that are always with us and offer words of praise to God for His never-failing power.

11. **Do Jews believe that Judaism is the only true religion?**

Jews regard Judaism as the only religion for Jews. But we neither judge nor condemn the honest, devout worshiper of any faith. Judaism is based on a number of ethical concepts: decency, kindness, humility, and integrity. These are regarded as eternal verities, but Jews claim no monopoly on them, recognizing that every great religious faith has discovered them, and others too.

12. **What is the most important idea in the Jewish religion?**

Judaism begins with God. "In the beginning, God created the heavens and the earth." This is the starting point of the Jewish religion, and all Judaic concepts stem from it. Basic Jewish beliefs concerning God are the following: God is all-knowing, all-powerful, omnipresent (i.e., everywhere), and all-good. Jews believe that they are morally responsible to God, who reveals His will to them. The duty of every Jew is to serve God's purpose in the world; namely, to help create the good life for ourselves and our fellowman.

13. Can you still be Jewish if you doubt God's existence?

God has an opinion about this question. According to the Jerusalem Talmud (Chagigah 1:7), God says, "Better that the children of Israel abandon Me but follow My laws." Thus, according to the rabbis, one can be a good Jew while doubting the existence of God. We are bade to incorporate Judaism's ideals into our daily living by studying and practicing Judaism even if we have doubts about the existence of God, because Jewish practice and study have spiritual and moral benefits in and of themselves.

14. What do Jews believe regarding why there is suffering in the world?

Although surely the Jewish people have suffered a great deal over the many centuries, I do not believe that God ever intentionally bestowed suffering upon them. Very often it is people who cause others to suffer. A life-threatening illness can also cause one to suffer, but I do not believe that the illness is the will of God.

Throughout the ages Jewish tradition has sought to capture and understand the meaning of suffering and pain. The Book of Job deals extensively with this topic, recording the spiritual agony of a man who has tried to harmonize his experience with his belief in an all-powerful and all-wise God. One of the book's many lessons is that a person's sufferings are a test of fidelity. No one is ever able to probe the depths of the divine omniscience that governs the world.

Our rabbis have always posited that it is not in the power of humans to understand suffering, especially the suffering of righteous people. Some experiences and events that we cannot explain must simply be accepted, with faith in the ultimate wisdom of God's will, and trust in the goodness of people and of God's creation.

One final thought. Judaism does tell us how to act when another suffers. Judaism expects Jews to care for victims—to comfort mourners, help heal the sick, feed the hungry, clothe the naked, house the homeless, and defend the oppressed. We are all to do our God-given part to help alleviate suffering by putting our hands out to help those in need.

15. **Where do Jews go to find God?**

Many go to synagogue to communicate with God. One of the great Hasidic rabbis, the Kotzker Rebbe, said, "God is where He is let in."

For me personally, the best place to go and find God and feel God's presence is out of doors. I so often feel closer to God when outside. I love to take walks every day with my dog, and the quietude of my walk is a spiritualizing experience for me.

16. **Has God ever answered one of your prayers?**

Many times. My first recollection of God doing so was when I was a child, saying a prayer on behalf of my brother, who was very sick with a bad cough and throat infection. I can remember putting my head underneath the blanket and praying to God for his welfare. And when he got better (and quite quickly!), I became an immediate believer in the efficacy of prayer.

17. **Do Jews believe in meditation?**

Yes, for certain they do! Meditation is a traditional activity in the Jewish religion. The Bible tells us that Isaac went out into a field to meditate (Genesis 24:63). You will likely be surprised to learn that Judaism produced an important system of meditation. Furthermore, since Judaism is an eastern religion that migrated to the West, its meditative practices may well be those most relevant to westerners. There is also considerable evidence that the Jewish mystical masters had dialogue with the Sufi masters of Islam and were also aware of the schools of India.

I have used meditative technique at Sabbath services with my own congregation. Many times we do guided meditation during our weekly Wednesday evening prayer service with our high schoolers.

18. Do Jews believe in the rebuilding of the Temple in Jerusalem?

Most modern Jews are in no hurry to see the Temple rebuilt, for they have no interest in returning to a time of sacrificing animals. Other Jews, especially some very Orthodox ones, continue to pray for the building of a third Temple. They study the laws of sacrifice and prepare those descended from the ancient priests for their leadership role should their traditional function regarding sacrifices ever be reinstated.

19. Do Jews believe in the concept of original sin?

Overtones of belief in original sin may be discerned in early Judaism as well as in Christianity. The biblical story of Adam's disobedience and banishment from the Garden of Eden can be interpreted as the basis of the idea for the "fall" of man and original sin. This is precisely how Christianity does interpret it.

The idea of original sin, however, was rejected by the vast majority of the ancient sages and the Jewish people as a whole. Jewish biblical commentators point out that the story of Adam attempts to explain how death, not sin, came into the world. There are two main reasons why the Judaic tradition rejects the doctrine of original sin. First, it introduces a morbid note which is alien to the Jewish mentality. Judaism has always had an optimistic outlook. The tradition encourages people to believe in their God-given power to rise morally and to achieve spiritual progress.

Second, it clashes with the belief in free will. The Jewish tradition has withstood every philosophy which condemns us to a predetermined fate over which we have no control. Jews believe that they are free to change that which is evil into that which is good.

20. **Do Jews believe in angels?**

The Bible and the Talmud are filled with stories about angels who serve as messengers of God. They are often pictured as singing God's praises in the heavens above. For me, and a number of my colleagues, any person entrusted with a mission and engaged in the work of God may be called an angel.

Belief in angels has never been a matter of Jewish doctrine. It was always a way of expressing the idea that God has many messengers to execute His will.

21. **What do Jews mean by calling Israel the Holy Land?**

For Jews Israel is the land of Abraham, Isaac, and Jacob, the forefathers of the Jewish people. Because the Hebrew Bible was born there, the Jewish prophets appeared there, and the great rabbis taught there, Jews believe that the land has holy status.

The Bible talks of God choosing the Israelites and commanding them to be a holy people. Thus, the fundamental Jewish belief that the land of Israel is holy land, for it was the original place where the Jews were selected for their special task of being a "light to the nations."

22. Do Jews believe that Arabs have a legitimate right to claim the same land that Jews claim?

The Jewish people base their claim to the land of Israel on the biblical divine promise made to Abraham. Jews settled the land, and even after the destruction of the second Temple by the Romans in the year 70 C.E., Jewish life in Palestine continued and often flourished.

Many Palestinians have posited that Palestine has always been an Arab country, and therefore the Arabs have a sovereign right to the land. The fact of the matter is that the twelve tribes of Israel formed the first constitutional monarchy in Palestine in 1000 B.C.E, and King David made Jerusalem the capital. Jewish independence there lasted for more than two hundred years, almost as long as Americans have enjoyed independence in the United States.

When Jews began to immigrate to Palestine in the early 1880s, fewer than 250,000 Arabs lived there. The majority of Jews have arrived in recent decades. Palestine was never an exclusively Arab country. No independent Arab or Palestinian state ever existed in Palestine.

Today's war between Israel and its enemies is over boundaries, terrorism, and the right of Israel to have defensible borders. Israelis and Arabs must find a way to agree on land ownership so that both can live peaceably and protect their own interests. With the recent death of Yasir Arafat, many people believe that the peace process can begin anew. There is much greater hope in the Mideast that the time is right for a permanent solution to the end of the fighting.

23. I know there is a Jewish calendar. What's different about it, and do Jews use the regular civil calendar too?

The Jewish calendar is lunar, whereas the civil calendar is solar. Since Bible times, the months and years of the Jewish calendar have been established by the moon's circuit around the earth. At the same time, they must always correspond to the seasons of the year, which are governed by the earth's revolution around the sun. In the year 350 C.E. Hillel II helped to establish a permanent calendar for the Jewish people that coordinated the lunar and solar years with each other. The coordination of lunar and solar phenomena ensures that the Jewish holidays will occur in their proper seasons as specified in the Bible (e.g., Passover in the spring).

There are twelve lunar months in the Jewish calendar with a total of 354 days in the year. Approximately every third year the Jewish calendar adds an extra leap month. The Jewish calendar numbers the years from the date of the creation of the world as determined by Jewish tradition. The year 2005 corresponds to the year 5765 (the Jewish year), which represents the 5,765th year since the beginning of the world, or symbolically, since the beginning of consciously recorded time.

Jews use the Jewish calendar to remind them of Jewish holidays, the time to light Sabbath and festival candles, when to celebrate the commemoration of a loved one's death, and the like. Most Jewish calendars are combined with a secular calendar, so that Jews will also be reminded of civic holidays and celebrations.

❊ The Bible

1. Did Moses write the first five books of the Bible?

The first five books of the Bible are known as the Torah. Since the Torah is also known as the Five Books of Moses, many traditional Jews believe that Moses was its sole author. By the time the Talmud was completed in the year 500 of the common era, some rabbis were already beginning to question certain biblical passages. For example, the Book of Deuteronomy describes the death of Moses, which makes it more difficult to believe that Moses wrote all of the books,

In the eighteenth century, a Frenchman by the name of Jean Astruc found that various biblical passages employed different names for God. He also discovered that when the passages containing each name were separated, two parallel accounts of the same story emerged. His discovery earned him a place in history as the father of the scientific study of the Bible.

Today most Bible scholars posit that the five books were the products of schools of people who contributed to its writing. Moses, of course, was one of the contributors. The material was gathered and edited over a span of many centuries, and that is why we find varying or contradictory statements in the books.

2. How do Jews view the New Testament?

For the Jewish people, the only Bible that is adhered to is the Hebrew Bible, known as the Tanach (an acronym for the three categories of books that make it up): the Torah, or Five Books of Moses, the Nevi'im, or Prophets, and the Ketuvim, or Writings. There are a total of thirty-nine books in the Tanach

Christians refer to the Hebrew Bible as the Old Testament because their New Testament is the second part of the Bible for them. Christians believe that it records a "new covenant," or "new testament," that completes God's "old covenant" with the Hebrews. Although Jewish students may take courses in the New Testament while attending school, for Jews the only Bible that is studied for religious purposes and as part of the Jewish heritage is the Tanach, the thirty-nine books of the Hebrew Bible.

3. Why did Abraham become the father of the Jewish people?

We cannot be certain why God chose Abraham to go to the Promised Land. No reason is given in the Bible, but clearly Abraham must have been a man of great faith to leave his homeland of wealth and prosperity and go to an unknown land. And he was a man of great charisma too, able to convince people to believe in a God who could not be seen or heard.

4. **For Jews, who is the greatest prophet ever to have lived?**

Undoubtedly it is Moses, the only prophet of whom the Bible says that he knew God "face to face." This means that Moses had an intimate relationship with God, and could easily access His attention practically whenever he chose to do so. He was also the person who led the Israelites to the Promised Land.

5. **Whatever happened to the Ten Lost Tribes?**

There is no reliable historical information on the fate of the Ten Tribes, but many legends have arisen about them. In the Middle Ages, when Jews lived under Christian or Muslim rule, stories spread about a vast kingdom, beyond the legendary Sambatyon River, inhabited by the Ten Lost Tribes. Some rabbinic authorities today claim that the Ethiopian Jews are descended from the tribe of Dan.

Over the centuries, the Jewish world has been periodically excited by reports of the discovery of the lost tribes in various regions. Eldad Ha-Dani, a ninth-century traveler, reported finding them in the mountains of Africa. Benjamin of Tudela heard of them in Central Asia in the twelfth century. The bottom line is that no Jews have been able to trace their ancestry accurately to any of the lost tribes, with the exception of Judah and Levi.

6. **The Bible describes a Jewish priesthood? Is there still one today?**

There is no priesthood today in Judaism that replicates the priesthood of bygone years. In years past the Jewish priests, called *kohanim*, were the ones who offered sacrifices on behalf of the people. With the destruction of the

Jerusalem Temple, sacrifices ended and prayer became a substitute. Today, Orthodox and Conservative Jews still regard the descendants of Aaron, brother of Moses and first High Priest of the Temple after the Exodus, as priests, with limited functions in Jewish life. Such functions include offering the blessing of the priests at religious services and receiving the first honor during the service for taking out the Torah scroll.

A Jew today who bears the name of Cohen, Kohn, Katz, Kahn, or Kaplan is probably a descendant of Aaron, but this is not always true. Some people have adopted these names to streamline more complicated surnames.

7. What are the Dead Sea Scrolls, and are they important for Bible study today?

In 1947 a Bedouin shepherd boy discovered some jars in a cave at Qumran, on the northeastern coast of the Dead Sea. The jars contained ancient manuscripts representing every book of the Hebrew Bible except Esther. Most of the manuscripts had been written about 100 B.C.E. and were in the possession of a group of Essenes (people who had split from the Jewish community in Palestine).

The scrolls are regarded as an important source of information about Hebrew literature, Jewish history, and the history of biblical texts. They also established the fact that the Hebrew text of the Bible was fixed before the beginning of the Christian era, and they have already made important contributions to critical studies and to translations of the Bible.

8. What is the oldest Hebrew Bible?

The oldest complete version of the Hebrew Bible still in existence dates from 1008 C.E. It is part of a valuable collection of old Hebrew manuscripts in the Russian Public Library in St. Petersburg (formerly Leningrad), brought there in the late 1800s. It is known as the Leningrad Codex.

9. **What is the oldest New Testament?**

The oldest complete version of the New Testament (as well as the Greek Old Testament) is written on parchment dating to the fourth century C.E. It is called the Codex Sinaiticus because it was discovered in a monastery on Mount Sinai in the middle of the 1800s. It was purchased from the Soviet government in 1933 by the British government for 100,000 pounds and is now in the British Museum in London.

10. **What does it mean when it says in the Bible "according to the Masoretic text"?**

Hebrew was originally written without vowels, spaces between words, or punctuation. The Masoretes were Jewish scribes who were active from the second century C.E. through the tenth century C.E. They devised a system of word, phrase, sentence, and paragraph divisions, as well as a detailed system for representing the vowels and accents on words. This ensured that the Hebrew Scriptures would be uniformly copied, pronounced, and interpreted.

11. **Why did King Solomon have so many wives?**

Solomon had the most recorded wives in the Bible: three hundred wives who were princesses and seven hundred concubines (female slaves). Many of his marriages were political. They were tokens of an alliance with a foreign king who had given Solomon his daughter in marriage in exchange for promises of peace.

12. **Who was the oldest person in biblical history?**

Methuselah was the oldest man in the Bible, living 969 years. However, he was not unique for his time. Jared lived for 962 years, Noah lived for 950 years, Seth lived for 912 years, and Enosh for 905 years. Adam, the first man, lived for 930 years.

13. **Who was the last Jewish prophet?**

Malachi was the last of the Jewish prophets (450 B.C.E.). He spoke about the abysmal conditions after the Jews settled in Israel following their return from the Babylonian Exile and became complacent in their land once again. This included the corruption and neglect of the priesthood and the neglect of giving to God. His book ends with a prediction of the prophet Elijah's return, which the Book of Matthew applies to John the Baptist.

14. **What is the Apocrypha?**

The name Apocrypha means "hidden," and it usually refers to a group of books added to the thirty-nine books of the Hebrew Bible. These were written between 200 B.C.E. and 100 C.E., and are considered by many Christians to be part of the Bible because they were included in the first Greek translations of the Bible. The Roman Catholic Church accepts twelve of these books, while Eastern Orthodox Churches accept four or five books beyond that.

15. **What is the Septuagint?**

The earliest Greek translation of the Hebrew Bible is called the Septuagint. Supposedly seventy-two translators (six from each tribe of Israel) were convened in Alexandria, Egypt, about 250 B.C.E. This translation was needed because so many Jews throughout the Mediterranean world only spoke Greek.

16. **How many commandments are there in the Hebrew Bible?**

The rabbis counted 613 separate commandments in the Five Books of Moses. Of these, 365 were stated negatively ("you shall not"), while 248 were stated positively ("you shall"). According to Jewish law, adult men must follow all of the commandments, while adult women (due to their familial duties) were exempted from performing positive time-related commandments. About half of the commandments are no longer applicable, since they deal with sacrificial offerings. About forty-five of the commandments, such as "you shall not covet," deal with a person's feelings.

17. **Who is Jehovah?**

Jehovah was the rendering of God's personal name that arose when the consonants of His name were erroneously combined with the vowels of its substitute in oral reading (Y-H-W-H and "Adonai"): *Yahowah.* This mixed-up form was never heard in the synagogue, but entered the English language through the King James Bible.

18. **Why is Jerusalem such an important city to people of many faiths?**

Jerusalem is holy to Jews, Christians, and Muslims alike. For Jews, it is the site that David chose as his capital city and where the Temple was built. For Christians, it is where Jesus ministered, died, rose again, and ascended to heaven. For Muslims, it is the place from which the prophet Mohammed was transported to heaven.

19. **What is Palestine?**

Palestine is the term popularly used today to describe the land that the twelve tribes of Israel occupied in biblical times. Its name comes from the name Philistia, the territory occupied by the Philistines in biblical times. By New Testament times, Palestina was a broader term, designating a recognized Roman province. Over the two thousand years since then it has been a popular name for the Holy Land. The British called this province Palestine in the early twentieth century.

20. **Where is Armageddon?**

Revelations 16:16 states that Armageddon is a Hebrew word, but no such word is actually found in Hebrew. Many scholars think it stands for Har-Meggido, "mountain of Meggido." Megiddo was the site of two decisive battles in the Hebrew Bible between Israelites and foreign forces, and might well have served as a symbol of the great final struggle between the forces of good and evil.

21. **Who are the Nazirites?**

Nazirites were people—man, woman, or slave—who took special voluntary vows "to separate themselves to God" (Numbers 6:2). The vow included not drinking wine, not cutting one's hair, and not going near a dead body. Samson, Samuel, and John the Baptist were life-long Nazirites dedicated by their parents (although Samson violated all of the vows). The Apostle Paul took a short-term Nazirite vow.

22. **Who is Lilith?**

Mentioned only once in the Bible (Isaiah 34:14), Lilith is included among the creatures of deserted places. In rabbinic literature, she is an evil night creature with wings and long, flowing hair. According to legend, she was Adam's first wife, but she was sent away because she demanded full equality with him. She took her revenge by trying to kill all newborn babies.

23. **What was the tent of meeting?**

In most cases, this was another term for the Tabernacle, the portable synagogue that the Israelites carried with them when wandering in the desert. Its name indicates that it was a place where people could meet God. There was also a separate tent called the tent of meeting (Exodus 33:7). This was one that Moses used to pitch outside of the camp, where he and the people could also meet God. The Mennonites have reconstructed a model of the tent of meeting in Lancaster, Pennsylvania.

24. **Did Elijah ever die?**

According to Jewish legend, because the Bible never uses the word "death" in connection with Elijah (and says he went up to heaven in a chariot of fire), he still continues to live today. On Passover Jews reserve a special cup of wine for him, even opening the door for his entrance during the Passover Seder. According to Jewish tradition, Elijah is the one who will officially announce the arrival of the Messiah.

25. **Was child sacrifice practiced in Bible times?**

Yes it was. Child sacrifice was a ritual practiced by some Canaanites, and by the biblical kings Ahaz and Manasseh. Evidence of the most systematic forms of child sacrifice comes from Carthage in North Africa, where the Canaanite Phoenicians migrated.

26. **Why does the Hebrew Bible forbid tattooing?**

Leviticus 19:28 prohibits self-mutilation of any sort: "You shall not make any cuttings in your flesh on account of the dead or tattoo any marks upon you." This prohibition was mainly because self-mutilation was practiced in pagan cultures. Today rabbinic law considers tattooing a desecration of the body, which is made in God's image.

27. **Besides water, what was the most common drink in the ancient Near East?**

Wine was probably the most common drink, since in the Bible it is described as something positive that marks both joyous occasions and solemn religious occasions. Jesus's first miracle was to turn water into wine.

28. **What was manna?**

The Israelites were provided with "bread from heaven" in the wilderness. It appeared each morning as a fine, white, flaky substance on the ground that tasted like wafers and honey. Its name (Hebrew *man*) came from a question asked by the puzzled Israelites, *man-hu?* ("What is it?"). Many botanists state that the extraordinary food the Israelites consumed in the desert has a biological counterpart that exists naturally in the Sinai Peninsula.

The substance was in the past believed to be an exudation of the tamarisk, but it is now known to originate in an excretion of two scaled insects that live in symbiosis with the tamarisk. The Bedouin tribes view manna as a great delicacy, harvesting it in June and July.

29. **Why was Moses not allowed to step foot into the Promised Land?**

Most rabbinic commentators believe that Moses was punished for his lack of judgment and faith because he struck the water (rather than speak to the rock as he was told by God). Interestingly, Christian Scriptures have preserved an ancient Jewish legend of a rock containing water that followed the Israelites throughout their trek in the desert. They compare the rock of Meribah to Jesus himself.

30. **What is a cubit?**

A cubit was the distance from the elbow to the tip of the middle finger of a grown man. It was the standard measure of length among the Hebrews. The standard cubit was approximately 17 inches long, while the royal cubit was longer, about 20 inches. God told Noah to build the ark 300 cubits long and 50 cubits wide. According to a member of my synagogue who is in the lumber business, it would have taken 40,000 tons of lumber to build Noah's ark.

31. **Did God really turn Lot's wife into a pillar of salt?**

According to the Book of Genesis, when Lot's wife looked back to see the rain of brimstone and fire befall the people of Sodom and Gomorrah, she became a pillar of salt. I have always doubted this story. However, when I last visited Israel I went to an area near the Dead Sea. Our guide took us to a nearby hill, and there, encrusted in the hill, was a figure that looked liked a woman. Our guide proceeded to tell us that this was none other than the salt figure of Mrs. Lot!

32. Why did God change Abraham's name?

Abraham's original biblical name was Abram, which means "exalted father." God later gave him a new name, Abraham, meaning "father of the multitude." This was to emphasize God's promise to Abraham that he would have many descendants.

33. What was the Jubilee Year?

The jubilee year was to come after seven sabbatical years, or every fiftieth year (Leviticus 25). It was a sabbatical year for the land (thus allowing two fallow years) and also a time when all land would revert to its original owners. Anyone who had sold himself into service (because of debts) would regain his freedom. The idea was noble, but there is little evidence that the sabbatical and jubilee years were actually observed.

34. Why did the priests perform many of their duties in the Temple while barefooted?

The priests were barefooted because of the sacredness of the ground on which they walked. God told Moses to remove his shoes at the burning bush because he stood on holy ground. Even today, when the kohanim (priests) in Orthodox synagogues ascend the platform to offer the priestly blessing, they remove their shoes.

35. **Were the Ten Plagues historically true?**

There are a variety of opinions and interpretations about the historicity of the ten plagues. Some commentators consider them legendary and interpretive, and maintain that the real thrust of the story was the release of the Israelite people by God, who chose them for a special mission. Other medieval interpreters assumed that these so-called wonders only appeared as divine interventions, but had in fact been built into the process of creation from its inception. Still others, such as the philosopher Thomas Aquinas, were of the opinion that miracles are events that cannot be explained.

Scientists have always been fascinated by the plagues. Many have come up with what has come to be known as the "domino" theory of causes—from the red algae that turned the waters to blood to the bacteria-ridden flies that caused boils. The plague of darkness was a sandstorm.

❋ Holidays

The Sabbath

1. What types of work must Jews avoid on the Sabbath?

Jewish law demands that certain types of work must be avoided in order to honor the Sabbath. The Bible mentions only a few, including lighting a fire (Exodus 35:3) and plowing and harvesting. (Exodus 34:21). The Talmud (rabbinic interpretation of the Bible) elaborates on the concept of work by listing thirty-nine categories of prohibited activity. These include writing, carrying, sewing, tearing, and cutting, just to mention a few. Rabbinic authorities today are not in total agreement regarding the degree to which these prohibitions must be observed.

2. Why do Jews light candles to usher in the Sabbath?

Jewish candlelighting time is at sunset every Friday. The Sabbath, like all the other Jewish holidays, always begins at night. The custom of beginning a holiday at sunset is based on the story of Creation as depicted in Genesis: "It was evening and it was morning, the first day."

The evening came first; thus each new day begins with the sunset of the one before.

Two different terms are used in reference to Sabbath observance in the Ten Commandments (Exodus 20:8 and Deuteronomy 5:12). In Exodus the commandment says "Remember the Sabbath day," while in Deuteronomy it says "Observe the Sabbath day." This led to the practice of lighting two Sabbath candles that would remind a Jewish family to both remember the day and observe it. The rabbis of bygone years encouraged the lighting of more than two candles, believing that increased light would add to the joy of the Sabbath celebration. Thus in some households a candle is lit for every member of the family. My maternal grandmother used to light a candle for each of her grandchildren and great-grandchildren.

3. **Why is the Jewish Sabbath on Saturday and the Christian one on Sunday?**

For Jews, the Sabbath begins on Friday night and extends through Saturday until nightfall when three stars emerge in the sky. For Christians, Sunday is the Sabbath. Historically, the early Church recognized Sunday as the day of worship because it was on Sunday that Jesus rose from the dead. Since the resurrection of Jesus is the focal point of the Christian faith and the confirmation of all that Jesus taught, the first Christians gathered to celebrate this event on the first day of the week (Acts 20:7), which is Sunday.

Undoubtedly, another reason why early Christians worshiped on Sunday was to distinguish themselves from the Jewish community to which many of them belonged before their conversion.

4. **Why do most traditional Jews walk to synagogue rather than drive on the Sabbath?**

Prohibiting travel on the Sabbath was an important contribution to preparing the day for its mission to sanctify life. The basis of the prohibition is the verse in Exodus 16:29, "Let every person remain where he is: let no one leave his place on the seventh day." This law was originally directed at the gatherers of manna, the heavenly food that fell in the wilderness. Travel on the Sabbath in Bible times, by riding on an animal, was also forbidden for the reason of seeking to avoid involvement in incidental labor, such as possibly cutting down a twig to help prod the animal on its way.

When automobiles were invented, observant Jews refrained from using them on the Sabbath. There was the possibility of mechanical failure and the prohibition of lighting fire related to the ignition of the engine, which produces a spark. For Orthodox Jews, the ban continues in force. Jews in the Conservative movement are allowed to drive an automobile, but only to and from synagogue. The use of a car for any other purpose is forbidden.

5. **Do Jews watch television on the holy Sabbath?**

Most observant ones do not. One of the work prohibitions on the Sabbath is the kindling of fire. Using an appliance such as a television has been deemed by some rabbinic authorities as synonymous with using fire. Also, the Sabbath is a day to be used to sanctify time. Watching television is not in the spirit of the Sabbath in the opinion of many traditional Jews.

6. What is the significance of the egg-twist bread that Jews eat on the Sabbath?

The enriched bread, often twisted, that is eaten on the Sabbath is called challah. It is first mentioned in the Book of Numbers (15:20). The Israelites were commanded to set aside, from the bread they baked, a small portion of dough for the sustenance of the priests. The word *challah*, usually translated as "cake" or "loaf," was first used in the Bible (Leviticus 24:5) to describe the twelve showbreads arranged on the altar in the Tabernacle. The twelve cakes were laid out in two rows of six each. According to most rabbinic authorities, this is the origin of the use of challah on the Sabbath.

Traditional Jewish households generally put out two challah loaves on the Sabbath table as a reminder of the double portion of heavenly manna that fell in the wilderness.

7. Is there a special Sabbath greeting used for one to greet a Jewish person on the Sabbath?

In fact there is. The greeting in Hebrew is *Shabbat Shalom*, meaning "May you enjoy a peaceful Sabbath." The Yiddish greeting on the Sabbath is *Gut Shabbos*, meaning "May you have an enjoyable Sabbath."

8. What is the purpose of lighting the braided candle that I saw being used at a Bat Mitzvah in synagogue on Saturday night?

The Sabbath ends with the ceremony known as Havdalah, which means "separation." It is the Jewish way of saying farewell to the holy Sabbath, which ends on Saturday evening with the appearance of three stars in the sky. Light has many manifestations, hence the benediction over light uses the plural "lights." The Havdalah candle, by having several wicks, produces a compound light and thus corresponds to the plural of the prayer. While the candles lighted on Friday evening symbolize the joy of the day that is just beginning, the candle that is lit on Saturday evening symbolizes a return to the workday world in which lighting a fire and performing work are permitted again. The Havdalah candle is most often held by a girl, and custom dictates that she hold it high, to the height that she would like her future husband to be.

9. **For traditional Jews, what kind of work is prohibited on the Sabbath?**

The Bible's concept of work applies to work involving the production, creation, or transformation of an object. One may spend the entire Sabbath opening and closing a book until one is exhausted and yet not violate the Sabbath. On the other hand, the mere striking of a match, just once, is a desecration of the Sabbath because it involves creation. Jewish law in the Talmud designates thirty-nine forbidden labors, including: plowing, reaping, baking, dyeing wool, weaving, tying a permanent knot, sewing, slaughtering an animal, building and pulling down a structure. The thirty-eighth forbidden labor is striking with a hammer, which means putting the finishing touches on a job, while the thirty-ninth is carrying an object from one's private domain to a public domain.

10. **Why is it the duty of a woman to usher in the Sabbath by lighting candles?**

According to the philosopher Maimonides, women are the ones to usher in the Sabbath because they are the ones who are usually at home attending to the household. The two candles are said to symbolize the twofold command of Sabbath observance: "Remember the Sabbath day to keep it holy" (Exodus 20:8) and "Observe the Sabbath day to keep it holy" (Deuteronomy 5:12).

11. Why is white the color of choice for the Sabbath dinner tablecloth?

The Talmud (Pesachim 100b) describes the custom of covering the Sabbath table with a white cloth as a reminder of the manna that covered the ground when the Israelites wandered through the desert.

12. Why is eating fish a popular Jewish custom on the Sabbath?

Fish has been a popular Sabbath dish for centuries. The eating of stuffed fish ("gefilte fish") has often been interpreted as a symbol of the blessing that the children of Israel would multiply like the stars in the heaven and the sands of the sea.

13. What is the prophet Elijah's role in the celebration of the Sabbath?

According to Jewish tradition, the prophet Elijah, messenger of the good tidings of the Messiah's coming, will not arrive on Friday when the Jewish people are busy preparing for the Sabbath, nor on Saturday when Jews are at rest. Consequently he is expected immediately after the Sabbath. The hymns sung in his honor express the hope that Elijah will appear during the coming week and bring the good tidings of redemption for Israel and all humanity.

14. Why do traditional Jews like to sing songs at the Sabbath dinner table?

Since the Sabbath is intended to be a day of rest and joy, singing is very much a part of its celebration. There are many special festive Sabbath songs, called *zemirot*, that are spirited and add to the joy of the festive meal. Clapping one's hands and stomping one's feet during the singing is also a custom.

High Holy Days: Rosh Hashanah and Yom Kippur

1. Why are the High Holy Days also known as the Days of Awe?

According to the Talmud (Rosh Hashanah 16a), God judges everyone's actions in the past year on Rosh Hashanah and renders judgment on Yom Kippur (the Day of Atonement). The awesome significance of these events gives these days the name Days of Awe.

2. Is it true that on the High Holy Days Jews have something like midnight mass?

On the Saturday night before Rosh Hashanah, it is customary to go to synagogue at midnight and recite the penitential prayers known as Selichot. Midnight was the time selected for recitation of such prayers because the psalmist wrote: "At midnight I will rise to give thanks to You" (Psalms 119:62).

3. Tell me something about the ram's horn used on Rosh Hashanah.

The shofar (ram's horn) is one of the oldest musical instruments known to man. In biblical times it was often used when kings were crowned and to intimidate the enemy in time of war. It was also used to herald the beginning of a new month. The shofar is sounded in the synagogue on Rosh Hashanah and at the end of the Day of Atonement as a wake-up call for Jews to ask forgiveness for their mistakes.

4. Why is Rosh Hashanah celebrated by some Jews for one day and by others for two?

In the Bible (Leviticus 23:24), Rosh Hashanah is a one-day holiday to be celebrated on the first day of the Hebrew month of Tishri. Many Reform congregations still observe it for one day, but Orthodox and Conservative Jews everywhere (including in Israel) celebrate it for two days.

The change from a one-day to a two-day holiday occurred in ancient times when it became evident that the precise hour of the appearance of the new moon for the month of Tishri could not always be ascertained. If clouds filled the sky, no one could witness the arrival of the new moon. Therefore, to be certain that Rosh Hashanah would be celebrated at the right time, the holiday was extended from one day to two days, thereby greatly diminishing the chance for error. (The Day of Atonement continued to be a one-day holiday because it would be incredibly difficult for anyone to fast for two successive days.)

Reform Jews believe that doubts about the certainty of the calendar no longer exist today, and therefore have retained the biblical practice of observing Rosh Hashanah as a one-day holiday.

5. **Why do Jewish clergy wear white robes in the synagogue on Rosh Hashanah and Yom Kippur?**

In Jewish tradition white garments are symbolic of humility and purity of thought. When the High Priest entered the Holy of Holies on the Day of Atonement, he did not dress in his usual golden vestments but wore simple white linen garments.

The wearing of a *kittel* (white robe) on Rosh Hashanah and Yom Kippur, not only by rabbis and cantors, but by congregants too, was encouraged by a statement in the Book of Isaiah that is recited on Rosh Hashanah: "Though your sin be as scarlet, they shall be as white as snow" (Isaiah 1:18).

6. **Kneeling is not a custom in the synagogue. So why does the cantor kneel on the High Holy Days?**

During the Musaf additional service, when the cantor chants "We bend the knee and prostrate ourselves before the King of kings," he kneels and touches his forehead to the ground. This custom was practiced in the Jerusalem Temple in bygone years by the *kohanim* (priests).

7. **How is a Jew traditionally greeted during the High Holy Days?**

The three Hebrew words of greeting are *Leshanah tovah tikatevu*, meaning "May you be inscribed for a good year." Used as a spoken greeting on the High Holy Days and also appearing on Jewish greeting cards, these words reflect the belief that God records the deeds of each Jew in the Book of Life, and thus one's fate is predetermined. But charity, prayer, and repentance can avert the severity of the decree.

8. Why do Jews visit a river or lake on Rosh Hashanah afternoon?

The ceremony is called Tashlich, which means "casting off." On the afternoon of the first day of Rosh Hashanah, Jews gather at a body of water to empty their pockets of their sins. They are asked to bring bread crumbs which symbolize their transgressions, and recite the verse from the Book of Micah (7:19): "And You will cast all of their sins into the depths of the sea."

My congregants enjoy walking with me from our synagogue to a small stream, where the Tashlich ceremony each year takes place. In addition to the casting of the bread crumbs, we also afford parents an opportunity to bless their children and offer a prayer for the year to come.

9. Are there any special Rosh Hashanah foods that are served during the holiday?

Generally, the fruits served on Rosh Hashanah are grapes, apples, and pomegranates. Apples are dipped in honey and a prayer asking God for a sweet year is recited by members of the family. Honey cake, because of its sweetness, is a popular dessert served during the High Holy Days. In addition, the bread served at the evening meals is round in shape, to symbolize the cyclical and eternal nature of life. Some commentators suggest that the round bread is meant to symbolize God's crown.

10. Why do Jews fast on Yom Kippur?

The requirement of fasting on the Day of Atonement is biblical in origin. The Book of Numbers (29:7) states, "And on the tenth day of this seventh month, you shall have a holy convocation and afflict your souls." In Jewish tradition, "afflict" has been interpreted to mean abstain from food. Children and any person who is ill are given an exemption from fasting on this holy day.

11. I have seen Jews walking to synagogue wearing sneakers on the Day of Atonement. Why do they do this?

Among the pleasurable activities banned on Yom Kippur is the wearing of leather shoes. (Bathing, eating, and sexual intercourse are also banned). The wearing of leather apparel was a luxury in ancient times, so it has become customary to wear rubber or canvas shoes (sneakers) on Yom Kippur to symbolize the day of affliction.

12. Is it true that worshipers beat their chests during certain prayers on the Day of Atonement?

A Jewish confessional, consisting of a long list of sins for which Jews ask forgiveness from God, is recited on Yom Kippur. It has become common practice for worshipers to beat the left breast (over the heart) with the right hand when saying the words "sinned" or "transgressed." The action of beating one's chest is designed to create a feeling of penitence in the individual.

13. Why is the Book of Jonah read on Yom Kippur?

The entire Book of Jonah is chanted in Hebrew at the afternoon service on Yom Kippur. This book was selected because it represents God as the God of all the nations. The concept of the universality of God is emphasized throughout the High Holy Day liturgy. The Book of Jonah also addresses another High Holy Day theme: that man can abandon his evil ways, accept responsibility for his actions, and return to God.

14. **Can you tell me about the fast on Yom Kippur? How old do you have to be to fast, can you drink water, and how long is the fast?**

Only adult Jews are required to fast on the Day of Atonement, Yom Kippur. For boys, this means being age thirteen, and for girls age twelve. The fast begins at sundown, and continues throughout the next day until it gets dark outside. The total length of the fast is approximately twenty-six hours. No food or drink is allowed. Exemptions include pregnant women and people who are ill. All other adults are required to fast.

15. **What is the prayer recited on the eve of Yom Kippur that nobody wants to miss?**

It is called Kol Nidre ("All Vows"), the prayer for nullification of vows made innocently or under duress. This prayer is repeated three times so that latecomers will have an opportunity to hear it.

16. **Aside from Yom Kippur, do Jews have to fast on any other days during the year?**

There are several minor fast days throughout the year on which traditional Jews fast. There is a fast day immediately following Rosh Hashanah called the Fast of Gedaliah. This fast commemorates the death of Gedaliah and the Jews who were with him. Gedaliah was the governor of Judea appointed by the Babylonians after Jerusalem's capture in 586 B.C.E.

Another fast is the fast of the Tenth of Tevet, commemorating the Babylonian siege of Jerusalem. There is a fast called the Fast of the Seventeenth of Tammuz, which commemorates the capture of Jerusalem by the

Babylonians. Traditional Jews fast on the Ninth of Av (in the summer), commemorating the destruction of both Jerusalem Temples. There is a fast on the eve of Purim to commemorate Esther's fast before she went to plead for her people. Unlike Yom Kippur and the Fast of the Ninth of Av, which are observed from sunset to sunset, the fasting on all other fast days begins with daybreak and lasts until sunset.

Sukkot, Shemini Atzeret, and Simchat Torah

1. What are the origins of the Sukkot festival?

Sukkot, meaning "Booths" and also sometimes called Tabernacles, is a major festival in Judaism. It is observed in the fall, four days after the Day of Atonement. Although Sukkot was originally an agricultural holiday, the Bible (Leviticus 23:42–43) ascribes historical significance to it by stating its rationale: "You shall live in booths seven days in order that future generations may know that I made the Israelites live in booths when I brought them out of Egypt." The booths that Jews build today are reminders of the forty-year journey of the Israelites in the wilderness.

2. Why is Sukkot called a Pilgrim Festival?

Sukkot, Passover, and Shavuot are called Pilgrim festivals, because on these holidays everyone Israelite was required to make a pilgrimage to the Jerusalem Temple (Exodus 23:17). All three of these holidays were originally agricultural, and in celebration of them the Jewish people brought their first crops of the harvest to the Temple, where a portion was offered as a sacrifice and the remainder used by the priestly families. Only after this obligation was fulfilled were the new season's crops permitted to be used as food.

3. **What are the requirements for building the booth during the Sukkot holiday?**

A sukkah is made of loosely assembled walls and has overhead coverings sufficiently sparse to permit the stars to be seen from within. The top of the sukkah that serves for the roof is generally made of branches, shrubs, and even slats of wood or bamboo. Decorations are often hung from the roof, including pictures, fruits, and vegetables.

4. **Is it true that some people sleep in the sukkah?**

Yes, some Jews take literally the words in Leviticus 23 "You shall live in booths." They interpret the word "live" to mean that one should eat and sleep in the sukkah. Less traditional Jews eat their meals in the sukkah but do not sleep there. Synagogues generally build a larger sukkah, where many more people are able to eat. At my own synagogue we have a very large and beautiful community sukkah. Last year we served kosher pizza in the sukkah, calling the event "pizza in the hut"!

5. **What are the lemon-like fruits that Jews use on the festival of Sukkot?**

The use of four species of plants is prescribed in Leviticus 23:24: "You shall take on the first day the fruit of goodly trees, branches of palm trees, and boughs of thick trees, and willows of the brook, and you shall rejoice before your God seven days." The Bible does not specify which trees and fruits are to be taken.

Rabbinic authorities have interpreted the "fruit of goodly trees" to mean the *etrog* (citron), and the branches of the palms to mean the *lulav*. The "boughs of thick trees" refer to the myrtle (*hadasim* in Hebrew) and "willows of the brook" are the familiar willow trees (*aravot*). These four species were to be held in the hand and blessed each day throughout the festival of Sukkot.

The etrog, the most important of the four species, is said to be symbolic of one's heart. The myrtle symbolizes one's eyes, the willow is symbolic of the mouth, and the palm is symbolic of the spine. These four together are used when praying to God with full enthusiasm.

6. Is there a connection between the Christian Palm Sunday and the Jews making processionals around the sanctuary with their palm branches?

During Sukkot services, worshipers carry the lulav branches around the sanctuary while chanting verses asking God for His saving grace. In Christianity, children who attend church on the Sunday before Easter are often given cut branches from a palm tree as a reminder that the people who stood along the side of the road when Jesus rode into the city of Jerusalem on the Sunday before his crucifixion threw palm branches on the road as they shouted: "Hosanna to the Son of David" (Matthew 21:8–9). This day is called Palm Sunday. The Hosanna that was shouted bears a striking resemblance to the name of the saving-grace verses recited on Sukkot, the Hoshannot.

7. Why are willows beaten during one of the services of the Sukkot holiday?

The practice of beating a bunch of willows on the floor or against the seats of the synagogue began when the final day of Sukkot became associated with the final day of the High Holy Days. Yom Kippur (the Day of Atonement) was regarded as the day that concluded the Judgment Season, and a new holiday called Hoshanna Rabbah was created to bring a close to the long High Holy Day period. Yom Kippur is the day on which God decides everyone's fate, and Hoshanna Rabbah (the last day of Sukkot) gave people one last chance for the evil decree to be reversed. Consequently, the beating of oneself on the Day of Atonement by pounding one's chest during the confessional recitation was carried over to Hoshanna Rabbah and the beating of willows.

8. **What is the holiday of Shemini Atzeret?**

Shemini Atzeret, the Eighth Day of Solemn Assembly, is often thought of as the eighth day of Sukkot. It is actually an independent holiday lasting one day, marking the conclusion of the festivities of Sukkot. It is prescribed in Leviticus 23:36 with these words: "On the eighth day you shall hold a holy convocation, and you shall do no work on it." The Yizkor Memorial prayers for loved ones are recited on Shemini Atzeret, and there is also a custom to read the Book of Ecclesiastes on this holiday. According to Jewish tradition, Ecclesiastes was composed by King Solomon in his old age, when he was depressed. Its contents, often pessimistic, was found to be an accurate expression of the mood of people who had just experienced a long period of holidays, from Rosh Hashanah through Sukkot, during which much soul-searching was required. Some rabbis suggest that with the joyous holiday of Sukkot about to end, it was important, by reading Ecclesiastes, to strike a note of seriousness to balance the gaiety of Sukkot. Shemini Atzeret also includes the chanting of a prayer for rain in Israel. The rainy season in Israel begins with the festival of Shemini Atzeret.

9. **What is the Simchat Torah holiday all about?**

Simchat Torah means "Rejoicing over the Torah." This holiday was celebrated in talmudic times, when the Babylonian custom of completing the reading of the Torah (Five Books of Moses) in one year was the prevailing tradition. Simchat Torah is only celebrated as a full holiday outside of the Land of Israel. Israeli Jews observe it as part of Shemini Atzeret, and so do Reform Jews.

Simchat Torah is one of the most joyous of the Jewish festivals. The concluding portion of the Torah is read repeatedly until all in the congregation have received the honor of ascending to the Torah and reciting blessings. Once the Book of Deuteronomy is completed, the Book of Genesis is immediately begun to be read anew.

On Simchat Torah, dancing, singing, and merry-making are part of the festivities. Sometimes the dancing is taken outside of the synagogue sanctuary into the streets. Children are often given little flags portraying Jewish themes and carry them around the sanctuary during the service when the Torah scrolls are also processed in a circuit.

10. **What do Jews do with their etrog once the holiday of Sukkot is over?**

Some Jews put their etrog in the refrigerator. It keeps the refrigerator's aroma very sweet. Others choose to make etrog jelly, to be saved and served on Tu Beshevat, the Jewish Arbor Day in the winter. Still others may turn the etrog into cloves, to be used for spices during the chanting of the Havdalah service at the end of the Sabbath.

The palm branches from the lulav are often saved until the following Passover, at which time they are used to sweep up bread crumbs during the search-for-leaven ceremony and to start the fire when burning the leaven the following morning,

Hanukkah

1. What is the story of Hanukkah?

Alexander the Great, the Greek king who ruled over Syria, Egypt, and Palestine in the fourth century of the common era, was a friend to the Jews. But when he died in 320 B.C.E., his kingdom was divided among several generals. One of them, Seleucus, took control over Palestine and Syria. He and subsequent rulers imposed the Greek way of life upon the Jews, including its many heathen practices.

In 165 B.C.E., led by the Hasmonean family of Mattathias the Priest and his eldest son Judah (called "the Maccabee"), the Jews succeeded in evicting the Syrian-Greeks from Palestine. Religious freedom was restored, and the Jerusalem Temple, which the Syrian-Greek king Antiochus IV had converted into a pagan shrine, was cleansed, restored, and rededicated. The name Hanukkah is a Hebrew word, and means "dedication."

2. Can you find the story of Hanukkah in the Bible?

The story of Hanukkah does not appear in the Hebrew Bible, known to Christians as the Old Testament. It is, however, recounted in the Book of the Maccabees, one of the fourteen books of the Apocrypha.

3. What was the miracle of the oil?

According to the Talmud, after the Temple had been cleansed and the priests were ready to rekindle the seven-branched Temple menorah (candelabrum), they found only one jug of undesecrated oil, barely enough to keep the menorah burning for one day. Miraculously, the oil burned for eight days.

This account is not found in the Book of the Maccabees, but it is the generally accepted reason for the observance of Hanukkah for eight days and the lighting of the eight-branched Hanukkah menorah. Biblical scholars now generally believe that the eight-day Hanukkah celebration is actually a "make-up" for the eight-day festival of Sukkot, which was not celebrated due to the war and oppression of the Jewish people during the fighting of the Maccabees with their enemy.

4. **How long must the Hanukkah lights burn? Is there a time requirement?**

The legal requirement is that the candles burn "until the time that people cease to walk about in the street" (Talmud, Shabbat 21b). Before the advent of street lighting, people did not usually walk about at night long after nightfall. In fact, it was dangerous to do so. Since the practice of the people was to be in their homes within one half-hour after nightfall, and the primary Jewish obligation was to publicize the miracle of Hanukkah, the practice of displaying the Hanukkah lights was designed for pedestrian traffic. Therefore, the rabbis who made the laws decided that the Hanukkah lights should last a half-hour after three stars appear in the sky.

5. **What family members are obligated to light the Hanukkah menorah?**

Jewish law specifies three options. At the very least, each household is to light a single candle on each of the eight nights. In the home of the more traditional Jews, each member of the family lights one candle every night. In the most zealous of households, each person lights one candle on the first night and adds one additional candle each subsequent night. Our practice is that of the most zealous, that is, we add a light each night of the holiday until we reach the required eight. Many families acquire a Hanukkah menorah (called a *hanukkiah*) for each person to light, although others light only one Hanukkah menorah according to this practice.

6. I have seen electric Hanukkah menorahs in hospitals and stores? Is this permissible?

According to nearly all rabbinic authorities, an electrified menorah may not be used to fulfill the obligation of kindling the Hanukkah lights. While electric bulbs undoubtedly give off light, the filaments are not considered a flame. Moreover, the requisite amount of fuel must be available when the lights are kindled. Because hospitals and stores have restrictions regarding lighting fire, the electric menorah is the only way to symbolically celebrate the holiday. That is why it is used in these places, but in the home a candle or oil Hanukkah menorah is the only way to fulfill the commandment.

7. Is it true that people should not do any work while the Hanukkah lights are burning?

Yes, the attention of people should be focused on the lights during the half-hour that the candles burn. And thus the custom is to refrain from working while the candles are aglow.

8. **What is the origin of the game that Jews play on Hanukkah using a spinning top?**

The spinning top is called a dreidel, or in Hebrew *sevivon*. Scholars conjecture that games of luck became attached to Hanukkah to reflect the "luck" of the victorious Maccabees over the Syrian Greeks. The dreidel spinning top has four Hebrew letters on it. The letters are the initial letters of Hebrew words that spell out the phrase "a great miracle happened there." This refers to the miracle of the victorious Maccabees that happened in the year 165 B.C.E. Players take turns spinning the dreidel and putting an equal share of something—nuts, raisins, coins—into the "pot." Players receive various amounts according to the Hebrew letter upon which the dreidel lands.

9. **Is gift giving on Hanukkah related at all to gift giving at Christmas time?**

Gift giving was originally part of the Purim holiday tradition, but not of the Hanukkah tradition. Some families from East European Jewish communities, on the fifth night of Hanukkah, gathered for a special family night during which the children were given Hanukkah money, called "gelt." Gift giving on Hanukkah today is in no way imitative of Christmas. Both customs undoubtedly originated independently of the other. Each had a similar desire—to add joyousness to the somber days of winter. It may well be true that Jews have increased the significance and character of gift giving in response to living in a secular and commercial culture that puts such a large emphasis on this tradition during the Christmas season.

10. **What are the traditional foods served during the Hanukkah holiday?**

In America, potato latkes are customarily eaten on Hanukkah because they are fried in oil, and oil symbolizes the miracle of the cruse of oil that lasted for eight days instead of one. In Israel, jelly donuts are the popular food during the holiday, because they too are fried in oil.

Eating cheese is another tradition in many Jewish households during the holiday. In the Book of Judith, part of the Apocrypha, Judith feeds the Syrian-Greek army leader Holofernes salty cheese to encourage him to drink wine. After he was lulled to sleep, Judith slew him. In honor of Judith's bravery, many communities feature cheese dishes on Hanukkah.

11. **Hanukkah seems like a Jewish Christmas. On it both Christians and Jews give gifts, and there is lots of light. So what's the difference?**

What both Hanukkah and Christmas have in common is the joy that each brings to the family and the desire to help the less fortunate that each holiday seems to generate. Although both holidays use light to the fullest, and share gifts, there are major differences. Hanukkah means "dedication," referring to the eight-day rededication of the ancient Temple in Jerusalem, which had been defiled by the Syrian Greeks. When the rabbis sensed that the military victory of the Maccabees might become the event most emphasized, they introduced the notion of the miraculous jug of oil that burned for eight days.

Unlike Hanukkah, which celebrates the Temple's rededication, Christians around the world celebrate Christmas as the birthday of Jesus. The word "Christmas" is actually a contraction of the phrase "Christ mass," which is a worship service to honor Jesus, known as the Christ child.

Although Christmas is celebrated each year on December 25, the exact day of Jesus's birth is unknown. Bible scholars have conjectured that he was likely born during the spring of the year. December 25 was supposedly chosen not by Christians but by Romans, the traditional antagonists of the early Church. Each year, as the days became noticeably shorter in November and December, Roman citizens feared that the earth might be "dying." With the return of the sun at the end of December, resulting in longer days, the Romans celebrated the Feast of the Sol Invictus, or Unconquerable Sun, on December 25. In the fourth century, a Roman bishop ordered that all Christians celebrate the birth of Jesus on that day. Many scholars believe that the bishop chose this date so that Christians, still members of an outlaw religion in the eyes of the Romans, could celebrate the birth of their Savior without revealing their religious convictions because their Roman neighbors were celebrating at the same time.

12. If Hanukkah is an eight-day holiday, why does the Hanukkah menorah have nine wicks?

This is a continuation of the practice followed when the seven-branched candelabrum of the Tabernacle and the Temple was lit. The seventh branch in each of these two candelabrums was called the *shammash*, meaning "servant." Used to light the others, it was not counted as one of the lights.

A ninth candle is also used on the Hanukkah menorah because the eight primary candles may not be used for practical purposes. By having a ninth candle to light the others, one will not be tempted to use any of the eight primary candles for such purposes.

13. Why is it permissible for traditional Jews to perform work on Hanukkah and not on other holidays?

Hanukkah is a postbiblical holiday. With the exception of Purim, only holidays mentioned specifically in the Bible became full holidays with restrictions on secular activities. Special synagogue services similar to those held on the three Pilgrimage holidays (Passover, Shavuot, and Sukkot) are not held to celebrate Hanukkah, although the liturgy has been supplemented with several extra prayers. There is also a reading of the Torah scroll on each of the eight days of Hanukkah.

14. Is there a popular traditional song that Jews sing during the Hanukkah festival?

Yes, there is. It's called Ma'oz Tzur, written by an unknown author between the eleventh and thirteenth century. This song, called in English "Rock of Ages," extols God as Israel's deliverer, which is the precise theme of the holiday.

Purim

1. Why do Jews observe the holiday of Purim?

Purim, the Festival of Lots, commemorates the deliverance of the Persian Jews in the fifth century B.C.E. by Esther and her cousin Mordecai (the son of her father's brother). Haman, second in command to King Ahasuerus, planned to annihilate all the Jews of Persia. He ordered lots be drawn to determine the day of the massacre, and it fell on the thirteenth day of the Hebrew month of Adar.

The plan was frustrated when Queen Esther made a successful appeal to the king to have the decree nullified. Thereafter the Persian Jews turned on their enemies and avenged themselves on the fourteenth day of the month. To commemorate the victory, the Book of Esther is read in the synagogue annually on the fourteenth of Adar (usually in the month of March). Families come with their children to hear the book read out of a scroll. They bring with them "greggars" (noisemakers), which they use to blot out the name Haman, archenemy of the Persian Jews.

2. **Why is the holiday called Purim?**

To determine the day on which the Jewish massacre was to take place, Haman cast a *pur*, which has been explained as a Persian word meaning "lot." Some authorities believe the origin of the word is Aramaic and means a small smooth object used to determine the winner of a lottery.

3. **Is it true that there is a fast day on the day before Purim?**

Yes, and it is called the Fast of Esther. It is the day on which the Persian Jews fasted to lend support to Queen Esther, who proposed to enter King Ahasuerus' presence without prior permission, an act punishable by death. She dared do this only because the fate of her people was at stake.

Haman, second in command to the king, had claimed that the Jews of the kingdom were disloyal, and planned, with the king's consent, to massacre them on the thirteenth day of the month of Adar. Queen Esther persuaded the king of the inadvisability of allowing Haman to carry out his plan.

4. Why are noisemakers used when the Book of Esther is read?

Called *ra'ashaneem* in Hebrew (and also known as "greggars"), the use of noisemakers helps to blot out Haman's name, which appears many times in the Book of Esther. Exodus 17:14 says: "I will utterly erase the remembrance of Amalek from under the heavens." Haman's ancestors were considered to be the Amalekites.

5. What are the various customs that Jews have on Purim?

One popular custom is called *mishloach manot*, which means to "send gifts." Thus a custom of sending money, food, and delicacies to friends, neighbors, and relatives. A special meal called a Purim Seudah (feast) is held on the afternoon of Purim. At this meal families often dress up in biblical costumes and put on a Purim "spiel" (play), which is usually humorous and very entertaining. The food that is most associated with Purim is called hamantashen, a triangular-shaped pastry filled with fruit, cheese, or poppy seeds. Some say the shape was that of Haman's hat.

Among kabbalists and hasidic groups, sweet and sour dishes are often prepared to express the dual nature of Purim, a holiday that shifts from a day of mourning and fasting to a day of joy and celebration.

Masquerading is also a popular Purim pastime. Synagogues have street fairs and Purim carnivals, where families dress up in costumes to add to the festivity of the day.

6. **Is it true that drinking alcohol is encouraged on Purim?**

Being a joyous holiday, the drinking of wine on Purim was taken for granted. The victory achieved by Esther began at a "banquet of wine" (Esther 5:6). Because of the great victory over Haman, letting oneself go and becoming intoxicated was looked upon kindly and even encouraged. Rava, a renowned talmudic scholar, said that a man is obliged to drink so much wine on Purim that he is no longer capable of distinguishing between the words "blessed is Mordecai" and "cursed is Haman" (Talmud, Megillah 7b).Today, because of the dangers of alcohol, most modern rabbis caution members of their congregations to be careful to drink wine in moderation.

Passover

1. **Why is Passover celebrated?**

Passover is a major Jewish holiday, one of the three Pilgrimage festivals. Originally Passover was two separate holidays. One was an agricultural holiday called Chag HaMatzot (Festival of Unleavened Bread). The other was a pastoral holiday called Chag HaPesach (Festival of the Paschal Lamb). Both holidays developed independently in the springtime of the year, in the Hebrew month of Nisan. (March/April).

The Festival of the Paschal Lamb is the older of the two holidays. In ancient times, when most Jews were still wandering shepherds, families celebrated the advent of spring by offing an animal sacrifice.

The agricultural festival, the Festival of Unleavened Bread, was a separate spring holiday during which the

Jewish farmers of Palestine celebrated the beginning of the spring grain harvest. Before cutting the grain, they would discard all sourdough (fermented dough used instead of yeast to leavened bread).

In the course of time, these two springtime holidays came to be associated with another event that occurred in the springtime, the exodus of the Israelites from Egypt. The Bible presents these springtime celebrations in this way:

1. The Festival of the Paschal Lamb (Exodus 34:25): This festival became identified with the happening in Egypt when God "passed over" the houses of the Israelites, sparing them from the tenth plague, which was visited upon the firstborn son in each Egyptian family. Passover (in Hebrew, Pesach), is derived from the Hebrew root *pasach*, meaning "to pass over."

2. The Festival of Unleavened Bread (Exodus 23:15): This festival, long known before the Jewish experience in Egypt, was tied to the hasty departure of the children of Israel from Egypt, when they "took their dough before it was leavened" (Exodus 12:34).

2. **I heard that Passover is observed for a shorter time in Israel? Is this true?**

The Bible commands that Passover is to be observed for seven days. After the exile from Palestine (70 C.E.), when Jews lived in countries throughout the world, an extra day was added. This additional day was necessitated by uncertainty of the calendar. The Jewish lunar calendar was based on the appearance of the new moon, which was officially announced after witnesses testified to its arrival. Since errors could be made when transmitting the information to distant places, an extra day of observance was added to Passover (and Sukkot and Shavuot too) in order to avoid possible desecration of the holiday.

Most Jews in the Diaspora today observe Passover for eight days, but Reform Jews and members of other liberal denominations follow the Israeli practice of a seven-day observance.

3. What is the Fast of the Firstborn Son?

The custom of firstborn sons fasting on the eve of Passover is based on the account in Exodus 12:21–28 in which all Egyptian firstborn were slain and the firstborn of Israel were saved. The angel of God passed over the Israelite homes, sparing their firstborn. To express gratitude for this, the day preceding Passover became a fast day for the firstborn male in each family. In time the requirement changed. The fast was excused if the firstborn undertook to study a talmudic tractate. In many synagogues, on the eve of Passover, the rabbi completes the study of one of the tractates of the Talmud that he had been studying. The practice is called a *siyyum* ("completing" a tractate), and it is followed by a celebratory meal.

4. What is leaven?

Five grains and anything made from them are considered leaven: wheat, barley, spelt, rye, and oats. Use of these grains is prohibited on Passover, with the exception of making matzah. The exception was made because the eating of matzah (unleavened bread) is mandated in the Bible (Exodus 13:7), and to make matzah, grain has to be used. Also, since matzah is made only from two ingredients, the flour of the grain and water, it can be prepared for baking quickly and will not become fermented.

5. **Why do Jews "sell" their leaven to non-Jews before Passover?**

All leaven must be removed from one's home and one's ownership during Passover. This calls for the sale of all such food and articles that one owns and of the subleasing of places where one has leaven stored. Because of the hardship this often involves, a procedure was devised whereby a Jew "sells" his leaven to a rabbi, who in turn "sells" it to a non-Jewish person with the understanding that the sale is only symbolic. The non-Jew is considered the owner of the leaven throughout Passover, but once the holiday is finished, it is understood that for some monetary consideration the transaction is to be nullified and the leaven once again reverts to the property of the Jew.

6. **What is the search-for-leaven ceremony all about on Passover eve?**

Exodus 13:7–8 says that "there shall be no leaven seen with you in all your borders." Thus, Jewish families conduct a religious ceremony on the eve of Passover in which the house is symbolically searched for leaven in every room. The procedure involves placing small pieces of bread in key places throughout the house, and then going from room to room by candlelight to find the pieces. Using a feather, the bread crumbs and pieces are brushed into a wooden spoon. In the morning, the spoon, bread, and feather are wrapped together and burned.

7. **Why do some Christian churches today celebrate a Passover Seder with their parishioners?**

On the evening before his crucifixion, Jesus took the unleavened bread (matzah) and blessed it. Since he used unleavened bread at his last supper, which Christians believe is the foundation of their observance of Holy Communion, some Christian denominations have chosen to have a Passover Seder.

8. **What is the Seder and why is it held?**

The Seder (meaning "order") is a Passover home service held on the first night of Passover and repeated on the second night by those who observe the second day of the festival as a full holiday. The original Passover service (not yet called a Seder) is described in the Book of Exodus: a lamb was to be slaughtered and then was to be consumed by families.

For many centuries after the Exodus, until King Josiah of Israel instituted reforms mentioned in II Kings 23, Passover was not celebrated as prescribed in the Five Books of Moses. After the establishment of the Second Temple, however, the celebration of Passover was revived.

The major celebrations were held in Jerusalem, to which Jews from all over would come together and offer a sacrifice of a paschal lamb, which they would then eat together with their families. Jews outside of Jerusalem celebrated the holiday by eating a festive meal. In time, ceremonies, symbolic foods, psalms, and songs were added to the celebration, which evolved into the modern Seder.

It is not certain when the first modern Seder was conducted, but it is believed that Rabbi Gamliel II, at the end of the first century of the common era, may have begun the tradition. It was he who said, "Anyone who has not said these three words on Passover has not done his duty: *pesach* [paschal lamb], *matzah* [unleavened bread], and *maror* [bitter herbs]." Scholars interpret his statement to mean that Jews are obligated to eat these three items and to recite the Haggadah, in which the symbolism of each is explained.

9. What is the book used by participants at the Seder?

The book is called the Haggadah ("telling"). It is an anthology of stories and biblical passages which recounts the story of the exodus of the Israelites from Egypt. The Haggadah was introduced by the Men of the Great Assembly almost 2,500 years ago in order to comply with the biblical verse, "You shall instruct your son on that day" (Exodus 13:8). Several thousand different Haggadahs have been published in almost every country.

10. What foods are on the Seder plate and what is their symbolism?

A Passover plate which usually has six circular indentations is placed on the Seder table so that the various symbolic foods can be displayed individually and prominently. They are pointed to during the reading of the Haggadah, and the symbolism of each is explained. The foods are:

Maror (bitter herbs), symbolizing the bitterness of being enslaved in Egypt
Karpas (a vegetable), symbolizing growth and springtime.
Chazeret (another bitter vegetable, symbolizing spring).
Charoset (mixture of nuts, apples, and cinnamon), symbolizing the mortar used to make the bricks for the Egyptian pyramids.
Zeroa (shankbone), symbolizing the paschal lamb sacrifice.

Baytzah (hard-boiled egg), symbolizing the regular Passover sacrifice brought in the days when the Temple stood in Jerusalem.

11. **Is the wine served at the Seder meal symbolic?**

Wine is Judaism's most festive beverage, and four cups are served during the Seder meal. Each of the cups refers to one of the verses of redemption in the Book of Exodus:

I will **bring** you out of Egypt.
I will **deliver** you from their bondage.
I will **redeem** you with an outstretched arm.
I will **take you** to Me for a people.

12. **Why is red wine the preferred wine at the Seder meal?**

Red wine is traditionally served as the Seder because the Talmud considers red wine superior. Because of the use of red wine at the Seder, blood-libel accusations were often leveled against Jews in the course of history. Charges were made that Jews drank the blood of Christian children at the Seder. Of course such accusations were entirely false.

13. **Is it true that prizes are given to children for finding piece of matzah that is hidden during the Seder?**

Yes, during the early part of the Seder a piece of the middle matzah is placed in a napkin or a bag. Called the *afikoman* (a Greek word meaning "dessert"), it is distributed to all the participants after the meal and is then eaten as a dessert. To make the meal more exciting for children, youngsters were allowed to "steal" and hide the afikoman. Since the Seder could not continue until a piece of the afikoman was eaten by everyone, the leader of the Seder had to search for it. If he could not find it, he would offer a gift to the children, and they would fetch the afikoman from its hiding place. In many families today the leader hides the afikoman and the children receive a small gift if they find it. When the afikoman is finally returned, the leader breaks it into pieces for all to share. The meal then continues with the reciting of the Grace after the meal.

14. Why is a paschal lamb no longer offered on Passover, as prescribed in the Bible?

The practice of sacrificing animals was in vogue only while the Jerusalem Temple was in existence. With its destruction by the Romans in 70 C.E., the sacrificial system came to an end, and prayers replaced it.

15. The Bible refers to a Second Passover? What is this all about?

The Bible (Numbers 9:9–14) makes provision for people who were unable to offer the paschal lamb on the fourteenth of Nisan by allowing them to do so one month later, on the fourteenth of the Hebrew month of Adar. Some people were unable to observe the holiday in the month of Nisan because they were in a state of ritual impurity, having come in contact with the dead. Others could not observe it because they were too far away from the sanctuary to arrive in time for the holiday. In either case, they would not offer the paschal lamb at the appointed time, and they fulfilled their obligation on the so-called Second Passover. I am told that there are some people who still commemorate the Second Passover by eating matzah on the fourteenth of Iyar as a reminder of the exodus from Egypt.

16. What is the origin of the Four Questions at the Seder?

The Talmud (Pesachim 10:4) mentions the four questions. However, the four questions in the Talmud are different than those of today. One of the Talmud's questions (which is no longer used today) was: "On all other nights we eat meat which has been roasted, stewed, or boiled, but on this night we eat only roasted meat." After the Temple was destroyed and sacrifices eliminated, there was no need for this question. So the substituted question was: "On all other nights we either sit or recline. Why on this night do we recline?" The new question was introduced because reclining is symbolic of freedom, which is one of the main themes of the Passover Seder.

17. What is the origin of Elijah's cup which is used at the Seder?

After the Grace following the meal at the Seder, the custom is to fill a special cup for Elijah, a prophet who lived some 2,800 years ago. Elijah fought against pagan idolatry, and in time his name became synonymous with the messianic age. According to the Bible, he did not die, but ascended to heaven in a chariot and then vanished. His return has been anticipated by generations of Jews ever since, and some believe that his return will mark the coming of the Messiah. The cup of wine on the Seder table that is reserved for Elijah symbolizes the redemption and the coming of world peace. During the Seder, participants actually go to the front door and open it, inviting Elijah into their home.

18. **Why is wine spilled from a cup when the ten plagues are recited?**

According to Jewish custom, a small amount of wine is spilled from the cup when the name of each of the ten plagues is recited. It is explained as an expression of sorrow for the pain suffered by the Egyptians from each of the plagues. In some households (mine included), instead of spilling wine, the custom is to take one's small finger and dip it into the wine, and a drop at a time is removed and tapped into the saucer each time one of the ten plagues is mentioned. The use of the finger is said to be a reminder of the verse in Exodus 8:15 in which Pharaoh's magicians, unable to duplicate the miracles performed by Moses, had to admit that it was the "finger of God" that executed these miracles that in the end made the liberation of the Israelites possible.

19. **Is all matzah the same, or are there differences?**

Machine-made matzah is mostly the same, no matter who is the manufacturer. However, a special handmade matzah (circular in shape) is also available for purchase. Called *shemurah*, or specially guarded, matzah, it has been watched from the moment the grain is cut to the moment the matzah is baked in the oven. To reduce the chances of the matzah fermenting (fermented food is prohibited on Passover), the matzah is prepared in moisture-free premises. During the baking process, all activity is carefully rabbinically supervised in order not to prolong the procedure needlessly, further reducing the possibility of fermentation setting in. The cost of this matzah is obviously increased by the additional care of preparing it.

20. **I was at a Seder and the leader wore all white? Why?**

The long robe, called a *kittel*, is the customary traditional garment for the group leader of a Passover Seder. It represents release from bondage and the celebration of a life of freedom.

21. **Why is salty water placed on the Seder table?**

In Jerusalem of bygone years it was customary at mealtime to dip a vegetable in salt water (as an hors d'oeuvre). Salt was used in connection with sacrifices because of its action as a preservative. Today, the salt water at the Seder meal symbolizes the tears ere shed by the Israelites in their oppressive condition in Egypt as slaves to the Pharaoh. At the Seder, salt water is first used as a dip for the green vegetable. Later, immediately before the meal, a hard-boiled egg is dipped in the water by the participants. The egg is a reminder of the holiday sacrifice brought in Temple times.

22. **Is there a book of the Bible that is read during Passover?**

Yes, the custom is to read the Song of Songs, which is a love poem expressing God's love for and courtship with the Israelites. Because of God's relationship beginning to blossom during the years that the Israelites were in Egypt, it is customary to read this book in anticipation of Shavuot, the day on which Moses received the Ten Commandments.

Shavuot

1. What is Shavuot and why is it celebrated?

In Exodus 23:16, the Israelites are commanded to observe the "Feast of the Harvest, the first fruits of your labors which you sow in the field." This festival is again referred to in Exodus 34:22 as the Feast of Weeks, the time when the first fruits of the wheat crop were harvested. Shavuot is the festival which commemorates the spring harvest. Over time it has also become associated with the time that Moses received the Ten Commandments atop of Mount Sinai.

Sometimes Shavuot is called Pentecost, meaning the holiday of fifty days. This is because it always occurs on the fiftieth day after the first day of Passover.

2 Why do many observant Jews stay up all night long on the night before Shavuot?

Jewish mystics were the first to introduce the practice of spending the entire night before Shavuot in prayer and study in order to properly prepare their minds for the holiday commemorating the giving of the Torah. This practice is based on an old legend which states that thunder and lightning kept the children of Israel awake during the time Moses was on Mount Sinai waiting to receive the Ten Commandments. The custom of staying awake is called *tikkun Shavuot*, meaning "preparing and perfecting oneself for Shavuot."

3. What book of the Bible is read on Shavuot?

The custom on Shavuot is to read the Book of Ruth. There are several reasons for this choice. First, the story of

Ruth takes place in the spring, at harvest time, which is when Shavuot falls. Ruth was the ancestor of King David, and according to a Jewish tradition, David was born and died on Shavuot. Finally, Ruth expressed her loyalty to Judaism by converting to the religion.

4. Are any special foods eaten on Shavuot?

The eating of cheese products on Shavuot is the custom. There are various reasons for this. One is that dairy foods (especially honey) should be eaten on the day the commandments were received on Mount Sinai because the words in Song of Songs 4:11, "honey and milk under your lips," imply that, like milk and honey, the words of the Torah are pleasant and good

A second explanation is based on the legend which suggests that when the Israelites reached their homes after receiving the commandments on Mount Sinai, they had little time to prepare a meat meal, since a good amount of time is needed to slaughter an animal according to the laws of keeping kosher. Instead, they quickly put together a dairy meal, which could be more easily prepared.

5. Why is the Jewish confirmation service generally held on Shavuot?

In the past hundred years or so, it has been customary to hold confirmation exercises on Shavuot, especially in Reform and Conservative congregations. The confirmation class is a group of teenagers who have successfully completed their religious school training several years beyond the age of Bar and Bat Mitzvah. Students generally perform a cantata at confirmation and lead services. Because Shavuot marks the giving of the commandments on Mount Sinai, the confirmation service works well with this theme.

❋ Life Cycle

Circumcision

1. Why do Jews circumcise their sons on the eighth day?

According to the Bible, Abraham was commanded by God to be circumcised as a sign of God's covenant. He was ninety-nine years old at the time and did his own circumcision in addition to circumcising his children. The mark of circumcision became a symbol for Abraham and his descendants that they would continue to follow in God's ways and obey God's commandments. Since that time circumcision continues to be performed on the eighth day after birth as a sign of the covenant, and not merely as a surgical procedure. The baby boy is also given his official Hebrew name at the ceremony, following the ritual surgery.

2. Does a baby boy have to be circumcised to become Jewish?

According to Jewish law, a baby born to a Jewish mother is considered Jewish whether or not he is circumcised. Failure of the parents to perform the religious obligation of circumcision does not alter the child's identity as a Jew.

3. **Who performs at a circumcision?**

Traditionally, it is the basic duty of every Jewish father to circumcise his son. Since few fathers are able to do this with competency, it has become customary to appoint a mohel, or ritual circumciser, to do this for them. A mohel is a Jew who is specially trained in the surgical procedures and customs and traditions related to the circumcision ceremony, known as the *Bris* or *brit milah.* Women too can be a mohel, although there are very few of them.

It often happens in smaller Jewish communities that no qualified mohel is available. In such cases a Jewish physician who knows the correct procedure and the prayers may be asked to perform the circumcision. It is customary in such cases to invite a rabbi to supervise the procedure and conduct the service.

Recently my alma mater, the Jewish Theological Seminary of America, has been conducting a special course in ritual circumcision for Jewish physicians. Both male and female doctors who are observant are encouraged to participate in the program. This will help to ensure that there will always be an adequate number of mohels in Jewish communities throughout the country.

4. **When and where does a circumcision take place?**

The Brit Milah ceremony is celebrated on the eighth day after birth, even if that day falls on the Sabbath or a Jewish holiday. Mornings are always preferable in order to show zeal in the performance of the circumcision, which is a religious obligation. Thus, if a baby boy is born on a Monday during the day, the Brit Milah ceremony should take place the following Monday morning. If, however, a child is ill and the physician advises that the circumcision be postponed, the circumcision may be delayed for as long as the physician deems necessary.

The Brit Milah may take place in the synagogue, the hospital, or the home of the family. Today, the home seems to be the first choice, since its environment is warm and most conducive to a family gathering.

5. **Who gets to come to the circumcision ceremony?**

Since the circumcision is a way if initiating a Jewish child into the House of Israel, it is appropriate to notify the entire community. Relatives, family, and friends (Jewish and non-Jewish) all enjoy sharing in the happiness of such an occasion.

6. **Who are the major participants in the actual circumcision ceremony?**

In addition to the mohel or Jewish physician and the rabbi, the following are the other participants:

Kvater: This is a German-derived word which means "godfather." His ritual role is to bring the baby into the room where the ceremony will take place.

Kvaterin: This is a German-derived word which means "godmother." Along with the kvater, the kvaterin also brings the child into the room where the ceremony will be performed. The godparents are often grandparents of the newborn, although aunts, uncles, cousins, and friends may also be used.

Sandek: This is a Greek term meaning "with child." The sandek's role is to hold the baby while the mohel or a Jewish physician performs the surgical procedure.

Elijah the Prophet: Jewish legend holds that Elijah the Prophet is present at every Bris. This is because Elijah complained bitterly (I Kings 19:10–14) that the Jews would become assimilated since they had forsaken the observance of circumcision. Today he is often considered to be the "angel of the covenant," and a special chair called "Elijah's chair" is used in his honor. The baby is placed on the chair prior to the ceremony. This symbolically enables the prophet Elijah to be present in spirit at every circumcision ceremony.

7. **Why is there a meal served following the circumcision? Is this a religious requirement?**

Jewish people follow every life cycle event, including the burial of a loved one, with a meal. This celebratory meal is considered an integral part of the religious event, and is a way of adding to the festivity of an important occasion. The meal itself has a special Hebrew name. It is called a Seudat Mitzvah, the term for a religious meal that celebrates the observance of a commandment.

8. **Are there any customs other than circumcision that commemorate the arrival of a baby?**

Yes, there are several lesser-known Jewish customs that are often linked to the Bris ceremony. Traditionally, Jews mark happy occasions with contributions of charity. This is a way of sharing the happiness of the occasion with others who are less fortunate. Some people make a charitable donation to honor the birth of a child. It is also common to give some multiple of eighteen dollars to charity, because the numerical value for eighteen is spelled out with the Hebrew letters for the word *chai*, meaning "life."

9. **Is there a penalty if a baby is not circumcised on the eighth day?**

Jewish law requires that a circumcision take place on the eighth day unless there is legitimate medical reason to postpone. If it should happen (and sometimes it does) that a baby boy is medically circumcised but the proper blessings are not recited or the circumcision did not take place on the eighth day, then a symbolic circumcision is required. This ceremony, which involves drawing a tiny amount of blood from the genital, must be done by a qualified mohel or a qualified Jewish physician. Non-Jewish adult males who are planning to convert to Judaism, if already circumcised, also have to undergo a symbolic circumcision.

10. **When and how are Jewish girls given their Hebrew names?**

Boys are named after the Bris ceremony on the eighth day after their birth. A girl is customarily named in the synagogue on a day when the Torah is read, although it is technically permissible for a girl to be named in her family's home or on a day when the Torah is not read. There is no prescribed time for naming a Jewish girl, but it is recommended that it be done as soon as possible after her birth, since one always hastens to perform a religious obligation according to Jewish custom.

11. **How do parents choose Jewish names for their children?**

The custom of naming children after other persons began in the sixth century before the common era. Ashkenazic (East European) Jews customarily memorialize a deceased relative by bestowing that person's name upon a newborn child. However, they did not use the names of a living relative because of the belief that a person's name carries with it both the power and characteristics of that person. Naming a child for a living person would, therefore, they believed, reduce and shorten the life of that relative. Similarly, they would often choose not to name a child for a deceased relative who had died early in life, lest a similar fate await the newborn. On the other hand, Sephardic Jews (from Spain and North Africa) often name babies after the living, usually a parent or grandparent. To the Sephardim this custom was an expression of honoring the living. Today, these two naming patterns continue as customs in Ashkenazic and Sephardic communities throughout the world.

When looking for a Hebrew name, people will often ask their rabbi for assistance or consult one of the many Hebrew naming dictionaries.

12. **When do Jews get to use their Hebrew names?**

Hebrew names will often be used in religious school, where teachers address kids using their Hebrew or Jewish names. They will also be used and needed when called to the Torah for a Jewish life cycle event. Thus, every Bar and Bat Mitzvah will be called to the reading of the Torah with their Hebrew name. Hebrew names are also required on the Jewish marriage contract, called a *ketubah*. One's Hebrew name will also be invoked in a healing prayer.

Pidyon HaBen: Redemption of the Firstborn

1. **What is the redemption of the firstborn ceremony all about?**

The Jewish people, like most religious groups, had special rites and responsibilities for firstborns. The firstborn of any species, man or beast, was offered to God. Whereas some ancient peoples offered their firstborn as a sacrifice to their gods, the Jews consecrated their firstborn, endowing them with leadership and special responsibilities.

The firstborn Israelite received the birthright, which made him the head of the entire family clan. Firstborns also played an important role in the story of the exodus from Egypt. Since the time of the tenth plague when the Egyptian firstborn were slain and the Israelites saved, the firstborn were to be consecrated to God. "For every firstborn among the Israelites is Mine. I consecrate them to Myself" (Numbers 8:17).

The situation changed when the Jews began their wandering in the desert after having worshiped the golden calf. When a Tabernacle was built in the desert, the special duties of the firstborn were transferred to the Levites, a priestly tribe, possibly as a punishment for the firstborn males committing idolatry during the golden calf episode. It was then that the Bible decreed that every father release his firstborn son from his special duties by redeeming him from a kohen (priest). Since that time Jews have followed the custom of releasing the firstborn male child of his ancient obligation with a ceremony called Pidyon HaBen, "Redemption of the Firstborn Son." This ceremony takes place on a day other than the Sabbath or a Jewish holiday when the baby is at least a month old.

2. **Who are the participants in the Pidyon HaBen ceremony?**

A kohen, the firstborn baby boy, the parents, and guests are the participants at this ceremony. In this symbolic ceremony, the father hands his son to the kohen and gives him five silver coins as redemption money. The kohen accepts the coins and declares the baby boy redeemed. A celebratory meal follows.

3. **Is there a ceremony like a Pidyon HaBen for girls?**

In recent years, Jewish families have created a personalized new ritual for their firstborn daughters. Called a Pidyon HaBat (Redemption of a Daughter), this ceremony shares certain elements with the redemption of the firstborn male ceremony, including a dialogue between the kohen and the parents, the exchange of coins, and a festive meal.

Bar/Bat Mitzvah

1. **What is the meaning of Bar/Bat Mitzvah?**

Bar and Bat Mitzvah literally mean "son" and "daughter" of the commandment. The Bar Mitzvah, and later the Bat Mitzvah, represents a Jewish rite of passage when a Jewish child reaches the age of responsibility for the performance of religious obligations, called mitzvot. According to Jewish law, these new responsibilities occurred when a boy became age thirteen and a girl became twelve.

2. **What is the origin of the Bar Mitzvah?**

The origin of the ceremony is shrouded in mystery and scholarly debate. The Bible neither mentions a Bar Mitzvah celebration nor gives any indication that thirteen was considered the demarcation line between the status of being a minor and an adult. In fact, when a particular age is mentioned in the Bible as a requirement or a test for full participation in the community's activities, the age given is twenty, not thirteen.

The Talmud is also silent with regard to a Bar Mitzvah at the age of thirteen, indicating that the ceremony as we have it today was unknown in talmudic times. Both times the reference is to any Jew who observes the commandments, and not necessarily to a boy at age thirteen. When referring to a boy of thirteen the Talmud uses the term *bar onshin*, "one who is punishable." This indicates that a child in talmudic times became liable for any wrongdoing he might commit at age thirteen.

The clearest recognition of thirteen as the age of responsibility is the statement in the talmudic tractate Ethics of the Fathers, which says that "at age thirteen one becomes subject to the commandments."

There are a variety of opinions regarding the choice of thirteen as the age of responsibility. Some ascribe it to foreign influences present in ancient Israel in the first century B.C.E. Others feel that it may be a throwback to the puberty rites practiced by many groups. Almost every culture in the world has some kind of initiation rite that heralds a child's entrance into puberty.

3. **When did the "modern" Bar Mitzvah ceremony begin?**

One of the first known scholars to use the term Bar Mitzvah in our modern sense was Mordecai ben Hillel, a thirteenth-century German rabbi. Most references to the Bar Mitzvah appear after this date.

It was on the Sabbath after the boy's thirteenth birthday that the Bar Mitzvah took place. The child was called to the Torah for the first time. And when the boy finished his Torah blessings, his father would rise and say, "Blessed be God, who has freed me from the responsibility of this boy." The text symbolizes the fact that from that day on the parent is no longer responsible for the child's misdeeds and the child is now responsible for his own actions. This was followed by a celebratory meal at which the Bar Mitzvah boy would often deliver a Bible-related speech to show what he had learned.

4. What is the origin of the Bat Mitzvah ceremony?

Beginning in the second or third century of the common era, Jewish girls who were twelve years old took on legal responsibility for the performance of religious obligations. As with age thirteen for boys, twelve likely corresponded to the age of the onset of puberty. However, girls were subject to fewer commandments than boys. They were exempted from a series of positive time-related commandments on the assumption that their domestic duties at home took precedence.

Many centuries passed before the Bat Mitzvah ceremony appeared on the scene. In fact, the first known Bat Mitzvah in America was that of Judith Kaplan, daughter of Rabbi Mordecai Kaplan, the founder of the Reconstructionist movement. As time passed, Conservative and Reform congregations adopted the Bat Mitzvah.

5. When are Bar and Bat Mitzvah ceremonies held?

In most Conservative, Reform, Reconstructionist, and Orthodox congregations, the Bar Mitzvah ceremony is held on days when the Torah is read. This includes Mondays, Thursdays, Saturdays, and all Jewish holidays.

6. **What do the Bar and Bat Mitzvah do in the service?**

Depending on the congregation, boys and girls may conduct all or part of the worship service, chant the Torah blessings, read a section from the Torah, recite the Haftarah (a selection from one of the books of the prophets) and its accompanying blessings, and explain in a short speech the significance of the Bible reading and Haftarah.

7. **How far in advance does a child begin to prepare for his or her Bar/Bat Mitzvah?**

Many synagogues in the Reform, Reconstructionist, and Conservative movements require five or more years of formal religious study along with a year of specialized Bar/Bat Mitzvah training. Students are strongly encouraged to regularly attend worship services as well, in order to familiarize themselves with the prayers.

8. **What happens to a person who never had a Bar/Bat Mitzvah?**

Reaching the age of twelve for a Jewish girl and thirteen for a Jewish boy automatically obligates them to be responsible for the performance of religious obligations. Adults who may never have had the opportunity to have a Bar or Bat Mitzvah ceremony will often have such an opportunity in an adult Bar and Bat Mitzvah class, often taught by the rabbi. Every two years a group of adult men and women in my synagogue celebrate a group Bar/Bat

Mitzvah, leading the service and chanting a portion from the Prophets.

9. Are Bar and Bat Mitzvah ceremonies always celebrated in the synagogue?

Usually they are, but they are not limited to one's local synagogue. Some members of my congregation have celebrated their child's Bar Mitzvah in Israel. Some of these took place in a synagogue, while others atop Masada or at the Western Wall in Jerusalem.

10. Can a person have more than one Bar Mitzvah during his life?

As a matter of fact, yes! When one reaches the age of eighty-three, it is customary in some congregations to allow that person the opportunity of celebrating a second Bar Mitzvah. This can provide a wonderful opportunity for family, relatives, and friends to celebrate an important lifetime milestone and ought to be encouraged. Several persons in my congregation had their second Bar Mitzvah, and it was truly a joyous and special occasion.

11. Can non-Jews participate in the Bar Mitzvah worship service?

The rabbi of the synagogue will discuss with the family of every Bar Mitzvah the extent to which a non-Jewish person may participate. There is usually greater flexibility in terms of participation in the more liberal Reform congregations. In most Conservative synagogues an English supplementary reading that is read by a non-Jew is often permitted.

Conversion: Becoming Jewish

1. What are the initial steps in the process of converting to Judaism?

In Conservative Judaism, the movement with which I am affiliated, there is no standardized conversion process. The same would likely hold for the other branches of Judaism too. However, some common practices are generally followed. The first step for a prospective convert is to have some initial contact with a competent rabbi. The prospective convert ought to be prepared to be asked many questions that will better acquaint the rabbi with the reason for seeking conversion.

2. How long does it take to convert to Judaism?

The time it takes to convert always depends on the conversion candidate's cognitive and emotional readiness. A year or more of study is quite common. Candidates are often required to attend a conversion school as well as private lessons with the sponsoring rabbi. Formal classes will assist in understanding the history, rituals, and customs and ceremonies of Judaism, while the personal meetings with the rabbi will enable the candidate to share feelings and reactions to the classroom learning.

In many larger cities throughout the United States and Canada, congregations have their own classes. In some communities a special conversion school is sponsored by a group of local rabbis or congregations. These schools generally have several faculty members and require both the non-Jew and his/her significant other, if any, to attend.

3. **I've decided that I want to become Jewish? How and when should I tell my family about my plans?**

There is no single approach to when and how you should tell your parents about conversion plans. Here are a few guidelines that might be helpful:

1. Tell your parents in person. Be honest and don't withhold information.
2. Pick a time that will be free from distraction.
3. Be prepared to defend and explain your motivation for conversion.
4. Relax and be calm. Reassure your family that your love for them is as strong as ever.
5. Discuss your desire to convert more than once. Most families need time to assimilate what is being told to them.

4. **How have Jews been known to treat Jews by choice?**

Finding a place in the Jewish community for a person who converts to Judaism may take considerable time. Obviously reactions will differ. Some born Jews will find it easy to accept a person who converts to Judaism. Others will try to be accepting but nonetheless may feel uncomfortable. Very often, though, born Jews are more tolerant of converts to Judaism if the convert's notion of what it means to be Jewish conforms to their view. In many cases, converts who actively pursue Judaism are more likely to be accepted than passive ones. Occasionally there may be guilt and ambivalence on the part of born Jews who feel threatened by a convert who knows more than they do and is more enthusiastic about Judaism than they are.

5. How do converts to Judaism spend Christian holidays with their families?

Converts and prospective converts are often confused about how to act with their parents and other non-Jewish relatives at holiday times. Prospective converts often have to grapple with such questions as the propriety of attending a family Christmas dinner or Easter get-together. Here again, there are no simple rules of thumb that will work for all converts and their families.

Some converts find it perfectly acceptable to visit their families at Christian holiday time and join them for dinner. They do this with the mutual understanding that they are joining their family as *they* celebrate *their* holiday. Other converts insist on inviting their families to celebrate Jewish holidays with them in their own homes.

With the passage of time and continued open dialogue, sharing religious holidays with one's non-Jewish family ought to become less awkward with decreased anxiety.

6. What happens on the day of the conversion?

When the sponsoring rabbi is satisfied that a prospective convert has acquired a basic knowledge of Judaism and is sincere about living a Jewish life, the final step leading to conversion is arranged. A Jewish court of three rabbis is convened at a Jewish ritual bath, called a mikveh. All male candidates must be ritually circumcised before immersing in the mikveh. If already surgically circumcised without the proper blessings, than a symbolic circumcision is required. In this ceremony a drop of blood is painlessly drawn from the tip of the penis to complete the requirement for entrance into the covenant.

The Jewish court asks the candidate a variety of questions, both factual and personal. Questions might include:

In what religion were you raised? What is your family like? When did you first entertain the idea of being Jewish?

The next set of questions usually deals with Jewish ritual, prayer, history, and the like. Finally, the third category of questions is geared to determining whether the candidate is prepared to fulfill the commandments of Judaism and abide by its laws. Some examples are: Do you freely choose, without any reservations, to enter the eternal covenant between God and the Jewish people? Do you accept Judaism to the exclusion of all other religious faiths?

Once the court decides that the questions have been answered satisfactorily; the candidate is invited to immerse in the mikveh (literally "a gathering of water.") Mikveh immersion is done without any clothes on. When a woman candidate immerses, a Jewish woman who comes along with her (called the "mikveh lady") walks her through the steps, while the male members of the Jewish court wait outside, listening for the recitation of the blessing for immersing in the mikveh.

Once the immersion with blessings is complete, the candidate is given a conversion document signed by each of the three rabbis. Some sponsoring rabbis also require the candidate to recite a Declaration of Faith. This is often followed by the conferring of a Hebrew name upon the candidate.

7. **How do converts choose a Hebrew name?**

Converts to Judaism are customarily referred to as the son or daughter of Abraham and Sarah, the first Jewish patriarch and matriarch. Converts may choose any first name they wish. Some look in Hebrew naming dictionaries and discover an exact Hebrew equivalent of their English name. Many female candidates choose the name of Ruth, since Ruth was one of the first converts to choose Judaism.

8. **Are there any biblical references to proselytes?**

During the biblical period, prior to the destruction of the Temple, the concept of conversion did not really exist. When Israelite men married non-Israelite women, they expected their wives to learn to worship the God of the Israelites and become full members of the tribes—and the wives did become members of the tribes. Similarly, when Israelite women married non-Israelite men, they joined their husband's tribe.

The Bible records many mixed marriages. David, Solomon, and Moses married non-Israelite women. Boaz married a Moabite woman, Ruth, who chose to become an Israelite.

9. **When did the first conversions occur?**

The first conversions occurred during the Babylonian exile (6th century B.C.E.) Many people were attracted to the Jewish religion and became part of the Jewish people even if they did not live in Israel. The prophet Isaiah referred to them as "those who joined themselves to the Lord" (Isaiah 56:3–7) and promised them that they would be a part of the historic return to Zion.

After the rebuilding of the Temple, Jews engaged in extensive proselytization. Even Roman nobility converted to Judaism. So too did Queen Helena of Adiabene and all of her royal family.

Marriage

1. **What does Jewish tradition say about marriage?**

It is a Jewish belief that marriage is a part of the natural way of life. The Bible says, "It is not good for a man to be alone. I will make a complement for him" (Genesis 2:18). God created Eve from Adam's rib, and with her creation the Bible says, "then a man shall leave his father and mother and cleave to his wife, and they shall become one flesh."

Marriage therefore is a religious duty and obligation in Judaism. And when a Jewish couple marries, it enables them to fulfill the obligation of "be fruitful and multiply."

2. **Are there any Jewish guidelines regarding the selection of a mate?**

The talmudic rabbis encouraged people to marry and always cautioned couples to exercise the greatest of care when selecting their partners. Guidelines include:

1. Hasten to buy land, but be deliberate in selecting a mate (Talmud, Yevamot 63a).

2. An old man should not marry a young woman (Talmud, Sanhedrin 76a).

3. He who weds for money shall have unworthy children (Talmud, Kiddushin 70a).

4. Do not marry a woman you have not seen (Talmud, Kiddushin 41a).

5. Do not marry a woman for her money (Talmud, Kiddushin 70a).

3. **Were the people of Israel always monogamous?**

Not at all. Examples of polygamy are found throughout
the Bible. Abraham had three wives, while Jacob had Leah
and Rachel for wives. King Solomon had seven hundred
wives and three hundred concubines.

Most of the biblical prophets discouraged polygamy. In
the year 1040 C.E. Rabbenu Gershom put a stop to the
possibility of polygamy among Ashkenazic Jews with an
important edict. Among Sephardic and Oriental Jews, the
practice of polygamy continued until recent years. In certain countries today, including Yemen in southwestern
Arabia, Jews are legally permitted to have more than one
wife.

4. **Why is marriage within the faith so important for Judaism?**

Judaism has always stressed the importance of mar-
rying within the faith and preserving its heritage of culture and traditions. Differences of religion often constitute an obstacle to harmonious husband-wife relationship. Even when mixed marriages endure, they often
impose a strain on the religious loyalties of one or both
partners, and cause difficult personal and family problems.

The earliest Bible story about the importance of mar-
rying within the faith is related to Judaism's first patriarch, Abraham (Genesis 24). Abraham sends his servant
Eliezer to find a suitable wife for Isaac, his son, admon-
ishing him with these words: "I will make you swear that
you will not take a wife for my son from the daughters of
the Canaanites among whom I dwell, but you will go to
the land of my birth and get a wife for my son" (Genesis
24: 3). This is the first biblical reference on the subject of

opposition to mixed marriage. Religion and family tradition are at stake, not ethnic or "racial" purity.

The strongest biblical denunciation of mixed marriage is found in the Book of Ezra, written soon after the return from the Babylonian exile. The practice of mixed marriage had become quite common then. Ezra did not simply denounce it; he ordered all intermarried Jews to divorce their gentile wives (Ezra 9:12).

Aside from the important consideration of marital harmony, Judaism opposes mixed marriage because it poses a threat to the future of the Jewish people, and to their faith, customs, and traditions.

5. **What's special about the Jewish wedding contract?**

The wedding contract in Judaism is called the ketubah, meaning "written." It is very special because its language is more than two thousand years old. Written in Aramaic (a cousin of the Hebrew language), the ketubah's important innovation was that it recognized that not only love, but legal commitment, is necessary to consummate a marriage. The ketubah specifies the husband's primary obligations to his wife. These included honoring his wife and providing her with food, clothing, and conjugal rights. The ketubah also specified a husband's financial obligations in the event of a divorce.

Originally, all Jewish marriage contracts were written on parchment and often artistically illuminated in bright colors. Over the centuries each country in which Jews lived included its own cultural symbols as part of the ketubah's artistic design. Today, the trend among Jewish couples is to have a handmade ketubah especially designed for them by a trained calligrapher or scribe.

6. **Who are the witnesses in a Jewish wedding?**

In ancient times, as today, the marriage contract is signed prior to the wedding ceremony. Two witnesses are required for the signing. Jewish law requires that they be adults, religiously observant, and not related by blood or marriage to either the bride or the groom. Orthodox rabbis will only permit men to serve as witnesses, but the other branches allow women. The ketubah is signed with complete Hebrew names.

7. **What is the symbolic significance of the wedding canopy draped over the couple at a Jewish wedding?**

Called a chuppah, the wedding canopy symbolizes the marriage chamber, indicative of the bride's leaving her father's house and entering her husband's domain as a married woman.

In biblical times, the meaning of the word chuppah was "room" or "covering." The Book of Joel (2:16) says: "Let the bridegroom go forth from his chamber, and the bride out of her pavilion (*chuppah*)."

Today the chuppah is usually a canopy supported by four staves which can be held by friends or relatives of the bride or groom during the ceremony itself. It can be a decorated cloth or even a prayer shawl.

8. **Are rabbis permitted to perform interfaith marriages?**

With the exception of Reform and some Reconstructionist rabbis who may choose to perform a marriage between a Jew and non-Jew, rabbis are not permitted to perform an interfaith wedding.

9. **Why do most Jewish brides choose to wear a veil?**

The veil is a sign of modesty, humility, and innocence. The custom of Jewish brides to wear a veil is often ascribed to the biblical story about Rebecca. When she saw her husband-to-be Isaac for the first time, "she took the veil and covered herself" (Genesis 24:65). According to still another interpretation, the Jewish veiling ceremony (called the *badeken*) developed to prevent a recurrence of what happened to Jacob in biblical times. Laban, Rachel's father, tricked Jacob by substituting his older daughter Leah, who was disguised by a veil. In order to avoid future dilemmas such as this, it has become customary for the groom to personally lower the veil over his bride's face.

The veiling ceremony takes place just before the wedding ceremony is to commence. It often will occur in a room where all of the guests are able to see the ceremony.

10. **What are the parts of the Jewish wedding ceremony?**

First, there is the circling of the groom. The bride circles the groom seven times (or sometimes three times). The origin of the circling is unclear. Some believe that its purpose is to ward off evil spirits. Others saw the number seven as symbolizing perfection, since the world was created in seven days. The preference of three circles is based on the biblical verse "And I will betroth you to me forever. I will betroth you to me in righteousness, and in justice, and in loving-kindness, and in compassion, and I will betroth you to me in faithfulness" (Hosea 2:21–22).

Next, there are two betrothal blessings chanted over a cup of wine which the bride and groom share. The sharing of the cup of wine symbolizes the affirmation that throughout the couple's life they will experience sweetness together.

Next, the groom places the ring on his bride's right index finger. This finger is used because it is the most prominent and can be easily seen by the two witnesses. In a double-ring ceremony, the bride then gives her groom a ring.

The rabbi generally will now read the ketubah, the Jewish marriage contract, and say some words to the couple.

Following this is the chanting of the seven wedding blessings. The themes of these blessings are gratitude to God for making man in God's image, and a request of God to grant the same joy to bride and groom as was given to Adam and Eve in the Garden of Eden. Bride and groom then sip from the second cup of wine.

The ceremony ends with the priestly blessing and the traditional breaking of the glass. The shattering of a glass provides a sudden mood reversal. There are many explanations for this custom. Some connect it with the destruction of the Temple, reminding us that even in time of joy we must never forget our people's suffering throughout history. Others take it as a reminder that marriage is as fragile as glass.

Following the breaking of the glass and the recessional, bride and groom will often spend a few quiet moments together alone in a room, sharing a food snack together.

11. **Are arranged marriages still popular in Jewish tradition?**

In traditional Orthodox settings, matchmakers are still used to bring couples together. Some are professional matchmakers, paid for their services. Matchmaking is quite uncommon among the other branches of Judaism.

12. **Why are candles used in some Jewish marriage ceremonies?**

Among Jews of the first century, the bride was received by bridesmaids, carrying torches, light being a symbol of purity. In later times, friends of the groom carried candles as they escorted him. The use of candles has been interpreted as a reminder of the lightning that pierced the heavens on Mount Sinai when God (the groom) accepted Israel (the bride).

13. **May a non-Jew serve as a bridesmaid or best man?**

Jewish law has no objection to a person who is not Jewish serving as a bridesmaid or best man at a Jewish wedding, since these honors are purely social. Nor would there be objection to Jews serving in these capacities at a Christian wedding, provided that the ceremony is held in a chapel from which Christological symbols have been removed.

14. **What is the handkerchief ceremony all about?**

Among Orthodox and some Conservative Jews, a handkerchief ceremony called *kabbalat kinyan* is conducted before the formal wedding begins. In the presence of two witnesses who have signed the Jewish marriage contract, the rabbi holds one end of a handkerchief and the groom takes hold of the other. Through this symbolic act the groom expresses his willingness to fulfill all the obligations the contract places upon him. In Jewish law, "agreement by handkerchief" was one way of sealing an agreement.

15. **Why do some traditional Jewish ceremonies take place out of doors?**

Holding an outdoor wedding, especially an evening one has long been popular among very Orthodox segments of the Jewish community. To them, this is a way of expressing the hope that the offspring of the young couple will be as numerous as the stars in the heavens.

Divorce

1. **What does Jewish law say about divorce?**

There is an entire talmudic tractate devoted to issues of divorce, elaborating on the specific details related to the Jewish divorce procedure. Jewish law requires the giving of a *get* (divorce document) when any marriage between two Jewish people comes to an end, whether or not there was a religious wedding ceremony. Technically speaking, Jewish law provides for a divorce action initiated by the husband, since it was always the husband who "gave" the divorce. In practice, however, the Jewish court on occasion would force a husband to give his wife a divorce under certain circumstances.

There are a number of specific guidelines on grounds for divorce. For example, Jewish law provides that a man can divorce his wife if she refuses conjugal relations, if she has no children after having been married ten years, if she commits adultery, and if she is lax in religious observance.

On the other hand, the Jewish court could force a husband to give his wife a divorce if he refused her conjugal relations, if he was cruel to her, if he converted to another faith, if he was lax in religious observance, or if he refused her support (clothing, food, and shelter).

2. **What does the Jewish divorce document look like?**

Originally the get was a document of twelve lines, written in Hebrew and Aramaic in Torah script with a quill pen on parchment. Nowadays heavy white paper is often used. The twelve lines on a Jewish divorce document correspond to the twelve lines of empty space separating the first four books of the Five Books of Moses.

3. **Who writes the Jewish divorce document?**

Any Jew is legally allowed to write a get. Since the get has so many complex rules, however, it has become customary today to have it prepared by a qualified Jewish scribe.

4. **Can you tell me something of the nature of Jewish divorce proceedings?**

To a certain degree, the giving and receiving of a get is a kind of reversal of the Jewish wedding ceremony. The entire procedure may take up to two hours. Most of the time is taken up by the actual writing of the document by the scribe. The document itself is retained in a permanent file. Official letters, called a release, are given to the husband and wife to certify that their marriage was dissolved according to Jewish law. Both are then free to remarry.

Death and Dying

1. **Why does Judaism not permit viewing the body?**

Judaism has a realistic view of death and dying. A person who dies is to be buried within twenty-four hours of the death. The more quickly a person can be laid to rest, the more dignified and respectful it is considered. Therefore traditional Jews do not permit viewing of the body, but it is sometimes permitted in more liberal settings.

2. Who prepares the body for burial?

Preparing the deceased in a dignified manner is a high priority. A special group of volunteers known as the Hevra Kaddisha, or holy burial society, prepares the body for burial, dressing it in white linen shrouds symbolic of purity and innocence. A watchperson stays with the body and recites Psalms, while the other members wash the body and dress it. Men (and women who follow the custom) are buried with their prayer shawl. In addition, earth from Israel is placed in the casket.

3. Can Jewish funerals be held in the synagogue?

Originally Jewish funerals were held in the home of the deceased, and not the synagogue. Today, funerals generally take place in funeral parlors, although some synagogues will allow their sanctuary to be used. The casket is generally brought into the sanctuary for the funeral service if the person is "important." Synagogues often define importance as having served as president, rabbi, or cantor of the synagogue.

4. Why do some funeral processions stop in front of the synagogue?

The practice of stopping in front of a synagogue and having the officiating rabbi chant a memorial prayer was commonplace in Europe and America before World War II. The custom, believed to have been introduced in some unidentified community during the Middle Ages, was undoubtedly based upon the desire to accord respect to a learned individual or a communal leader. Today the practice of stopping in front of a synagogue is still possible, but not often followed.

5. **Why do Jews generally not use metal caskets?**

Some mourners are tempted to purchase a casket that "will last forever," but Jewish tradition follows the lead in the text "for dust you are and to dust you shall return" (Genesis 3:19). In other words, whatever prevents the process of returning to dust is considered inconsistent with traditional Jewish practice. That is why the casket must be made entirely of wood.

6. **Are Jewish people buried in special garments?**

Traditional Jews choose to be buried in shrouds, white garments made of linen (or sometimes muslin or cotton). All such garments are alike in order to ensure that everyone, regardless of socio-economic status, is equal at death. Instead of frantically searching for the deceased's finest clothes, with everyone having an opinion or a favorite outfit, these simple garments are donned by the deceased to ensure the democratic principle and avoid potential problems.

7. **What is the Jewish definition of an official mourner?**

According to Jewish law, one is required to observe the laws of mourning for seven relatives: father, mother, spouse, son, daughter, sister, and brother.

8. Why do Jews generally not bring flowers to a funeral?

Jewish practice encourages well-wishers to donate to charity in memory of the deceased, and therefore the use of flowers is discouraged. (Sephardic custom allows for flowers.)

9. Is it true that mourners tear their clothes when learning of the death of a loved one?

Yes, one of the most striking Jewish expressions of grief is "cutting," called *keriah*. This ceremony is known as the rending of the garments, an opportunity for psychological relief, allowing the mourner to express anguish and anger by means of an act of destruction made sacred by Jewish tradition.

Tearing is considered an outward sign of grief and an acceptance of death. The custom originated with Jacob, David, and Job in Bible times. All of them cut their clothing after experiencing the death of a loved one. For a deceased parent, the cutting is customarily on the left side, closest to the heart. For all others, the cutting is done on the right side. Today a black ribbon is often cut rather than one's actual clothing.

10. Why is the backside of the shovel used to fill in the grave at a funeral?

The reason for using the back side of a shovel to fill in a grave is obscure and probably started as a local custom. The custom may have been instituted to establish a difference between the ordinary type of shoveling to fill in a hole and the occasion of shoveling earth to bury a loved one.

11. I was once at the burial of an Orthodox Jew and everyone filled in the grave with earth? Is this the normal custom for everyone?

Orthodox Jews believe in filling the entire grave with earth before leaving the cemetery. In most other cases, the usual custom is to have every person at the burial take several shovelfuls of earth and place it in the grave. The act of burying the dead is considered an act of *hesed* (extreme kindness).

12. Why do those at the graveside form two rows at the conclusion of the service?

The ancient custom requiring those attending a funeral to form two rows at the conclusion of the service goes back to talmudic times. The mourners pass through the rows in order to receive the words of consolation uttered in Hebrew, "May God comfort you along with all the mourners of Zion and Jerusalem."

13. What is Shivah?

Shivah, taken from the Hebrew word for "seven," refers to the first seven days of mourning. It begins after the deceased has been interred and then usually lasts for seven days. In Judaism, there is always a creative tension between personal and communal joy and sorrow. This pull is felt at various times and seasons during the year when a death occurs.

Actual Shivah is divided into two parts. The first three days following the interment are a period of intense grief. Some Reform and Reconstructionist rabbis have abbreviated Shivah to this period only. During the first three days, Jewish tradition requires that the bereaved stay at home.

Friends are encouraged to visit and worship services often take place in the home of the bereaved as well. Among more traditional Jews, shaving and personal grooming (but not hygienic practices) are avoided. Mirrors are covered in the house of the bereaved, since mourners are expected to focus on their relationship with the deceased and not on personal vanity. Mourners generally sit on low stools or boxes, and do not wear leather shoes, a sign of luxury. A candle (which lasts throughout the seven-day period) is kindled in the house of the bereaved.

14. Why are round foods served at the home of the bereaved upon returning from the cemetery?

This meal, called the "meal of consolation," is often made up of hard-boiled eggs (symbol of eternal renewal and life), cooked vegetables (lentils), and a beverage—all symbols of the cyclical nature of life.

15. Are there any customs related to the end of the Shivah period?

When mourners "get up" from Shivah, they customarily walk a short distance, usually around the block, to symbolize their return to society and the real world, from which death has forced them to withdraw. The mourners now enter a second phase of mourning, called Sheloshim ("thirty"). During the next three weeks they are allowed to return to a normal daily routine, but entertainment is avoided.

16. What is the Mourner's Kaddish?

The Kaddish ("Sanctification") prayer recited by mourners has no reference to death. Rather, it is a strong statement of faith, proclaiming the glory of God's name. The Mourner's Kaddish is said by the bereaved each time he or she visits the synagogue throughout the year. All mourners rise when the prayer is recited, as do people who are commemorating the anniversary of the death of a loved one.

17. **What is an unveiling?**

In Western countries and in America it is customary to consecrate the tombstone with a service. In America this ritual is called the unveiling because the tombstone is covered with a cloth that is removed by the family during the service.

The unveiling ceremony takes place within a year after the death. It offers an opportunity for the family to pay tribute to their loved one. Immediate family and close friends generally are among those who attend. Although there is often a rabbi to officiate, many times family members conduct their own service. Most unveilings consist of reading psalms, some brief remarks about the deceased, a prayer asking God to rest the deceased's soul in peace, and the recitation of the Mourner's Kaddish. When the ceremony ends, it is customary for each person to place a small pebble or stone on the gravestone. Laying stones on monuments is a sign that someone has visited the cemetery and thus an acknowledgment that the deceased is still loved and remembered.

18. **What is generally written on a Jewish gravestone?**

Usually the deceased's Hebrew name, the dates of birth and death according to the Hebrew calendar, and the expression "here rests" appear on the tombstone. For Jews who are from the priestly tribe, an engraving of hands raised in the Priestly Benediction is the norm. A Levite's tombstone will often have a ewer carved out over the inscriptions as a symbol of his office, because in ancient times the Levites washed the priest's hands before he gave the Priestly Benediction. Occasionally there will be a verse from the Bible or rabbinic literature on the tombstone.

19. **What do Jews do on the anniversary of the death of a loved one?**

Jewish tradition has added an additional ritual to help meet the crisis of bereavement. This is the annual commemoration of the anniversary of death known as Yahrzeit, a Yiddish name meaning "year time." Each year, on the anniversary of the death, Jews consecrate a special day of remembrance for their loved one. The commemoration begins with the lighting of a twenty-four-hour candle on the night of the anniversary, "The soul of a person," says the Book of Proverbs (20:27), "is the lamp of God."

On the actual day of the Yahrzeit, it is customary to attend services and recite the Mourner's Kaddish and the prayer for resting the soul (Eil Malei Rachamim). Also appropriate is the fulfillment of some good deed in honor of the deceased, such as contributing to a worthy cause. It is also appropriate for family and friends to gather on the Yahrzeit for the purpose of recalling various aspects of the life of the deceased, perpetuating his or her memory in a warm and loving family atmosphere.

20. **What are the other special times that Jews are to remember their loved ones?**

On Yom Kippur (Day of Atonement) and on the pilgrimage holidays, there is a remembrance service called Yizkor ("Remember"). Participants in this service are enabled to remember their loved ones and the values they cherished. Yizkor may be said for parents, grandparents, husbands and wives, children, family, and friends, both Jewish and non-Jewish. As with Yahrzeit, it is customary to kindle a twenty-four-hour candle on the evening preceding Yizkor. Mourners also customarily pledge charity and perform other loving deeds of kindness to honor the memory of their beloved departed.

21. Can Jews be buried in mausoleums?

Since the requirement to inter the deceased refers specifically to burial in the earth, a mausoleum built over a burial plot is permissible. Mausoleums in which the casket is kept above the earth are contrary to the biblical directive that emphasizes earthly burial, but liberal Jews permit them.

22. Do Jews cremate?

While liberal Judaism allows cremation, it is traditionally prohibited because the body cannot return naturally to the earth. According to this perspective, if a cremation does take place, the ashes would not be buried in a Jewish cemetery. Some cemeteries will allow burial of ashes, however, and in this way we preserve some attachment to the Jewish community by allowing for burial in Jewishly consecrated soil.

Jewish mourning practices serve both to honor the deceased and comfort the bereaved. Generally, cremation provides for neither.

23. **What does Jewish law say regarding amputated limbs?**

If a Jew dies with severed limbs, they must be buried with the deceased. Previously amputated limbs should be buried in the eventual grave of the individual or in a family plot nearby.

24. **What is the Jewish belief regarding life after death?**

Traditional Judaism subscribes to a future life and a world-to-come. Jews have many different ways of understanding immortality. Here is a summary:

Influence through family: We live on through the lives of our family and descendants. Eternal life occurs biologically through the children one brings into the world.

Immortality through influence: We live on by influencing others.

Influence through deeds: We live on through our deeds and creative work.

Influence through memory: We live on in the memory of those who knew and loved us.

Reincarnation: The mystics and kabbalists believed that our souls return again and again in different bodies.

Resurrection: This is the belief that the physical body will be resurrected during the messianic era.

25. **Can non-Jews be buried in a Jewish cemetery?**

The Orthodox prohibit burying a non-Jewish spouse in a Jewish cemetery. Some Jewish cemeteries permit non-Jews to be buried in them.

26. **Can non-Jews act as pallbearers?**

Although Jewish law does not prohibit non-Jews from acting as pallbearers, it is traditional for only family members and close Jewish friends to carry the deceased to his or her final resting place.

✳ Dietary Laws

1. What does the word "kosher" mean?

The word "kosher" means ritually fit or proper. Food that is kosher is food that a Jews is able to eat because it meets the criteria of being ritually fit.

2. What is the purpose of the dietary laws?

The Bible (Leviticus 11:45) offers a single reason for the dietary laws: to help Israel become a holy nation. By following a distinctive diet, Israel was encouraged to remain apart, separate from its idol-worshiping neighbors. This lifestyle ensured that the adoption of idolatrous ways by Jews would be kept to a minimum.

The medieval philosopher Maimonides is one of a number of authorities who viewed the dietary laws as having health value and as being a vehicle to teach compassion. These points are not made in the Bible.

3. Is killing animals the kosher way less painful for animals?

Judaism has a distinguished record on the proper treatment of animals. It is an absolute requirement, when slaughtering an animal, that pain and suffering be minimized. Thus, the laws of keeping kosher require that the knife be extremely sharp so that the animal's death occurs quickly and painlessly.

4. **What do the little letters on food packages mean, signifying food is kosher?**

Various organizations, in cooperation with Orthodox rabbis, supervise the manufacture of and processing of thousands of different kosher products and foods. A company wishing to have its food certified as kosher must apply to one of these organizations. The organization carefully investigates the manufacturing techniques and ingredients to determine whether they meet the standards of the certifying organization. More than a hundred organizations nationwide and in Canada offer rabbinic certification, and each has its own symbol that appears on the food products it certifies. One of the largest of these organizations is the Union of Orthodox Congregations. It is known as the OU, and its symbol is a *U* with a circle around it. Some kosher products carry the letter *K* on their packaging to indicate that they are under rabbinic supervision but not necessarily Orthodox supervision.

5. **I once ate in a glatt kosher restaurant? What does "glatt kosher" mean?**

The word *glatt* is a Yiddish word that means "smooth." In talmudic law it referred to the lungs of an animal. If the lung of a slaughtered animal was found to be scarred or damaged, the meat of that animal was considered nonkosher.

Today it is common to find fish, candy, and even diary products with the stamp of glatt on them. It is technically inaccurate to do this, since glatt specifically relates to animal foods.

6. **Why are people who keep kosher not allowed to eat shrimp or shellfish?**

Leviticus 11:44–45 describes all of the forbidden fowl, animals, and fish that are not permissible. Fish that are kosher must have fins and scales. This eliminates shrimp and shellfish from a kosher diet.

7. **Why do Jews who keep kosher not eat cheeseburgers?**

In the Book of Deuteronomy (14:21) and the Book of Exodus (23:19) the following command is set forth: "You shall not cook a kid in its mother's milk." From this commandment, later generations of scholars drew the conclusion that any mixing of meat and milk, whether in cooking or in serving, is a violation of the laws of keeping kosher. Apparently pagan custom in biblical times was to cook a kid in its mother's milk, which obviously displayed a lack of compassion toward the mother of the kid.

8. **Is hunting permitted according to Jewish tradition?**

Animals killed by hunters, even kosher ones (those that have split hooves and chew their cud), are considered unkosher. If a kosher animal, such as a deer, is trapped but not injured, its flesh may be eaten if the animal is killed by a qualified Jewish ritual slaughterer in the prescribed ritual manner. The Talmud (Chullin 60b) discourages hunting, especially for sport. It is placed in the category of cruelty to animals, a practice condemned in the Bible.

9. **Why are animals that chew the cud and have split hooves kosher, while others are not?**

The Bible gives no reason why only animals with split hooves and that chew the cud are kosher. Nor does it explain why certain fish and certain are kosher, while others are not. All explanations are purely speculative.

10. **What makes wine kosher?**

The Talmud indicates that wine to be used in connection with idolatrous worship was absolutely forbidden to Jews. Later, this prohibition was extended to include all wine touched by non-Jews, even if the wine was made specifically for Jewish use.

Today it is generally presumed that Christians and Muslims are not idolaters, and wine handled by them may be used. Nevertheless, many members of the Orthodox community do not use such wine under any circumstances, while others will use it only if it has been pre-boiled.

11. **Why is there such an aversion to eating pig?**

The special aversion of Jews to the flesh of the swine goes back to the Hasmonean period in Jewish history (second century before the common era), when the Syrian Greeks who had occupied Palestine tried to force Jews to sacrifice pigs in the Temple and eat their flesh. The Talmud says, "Cursed is the one who raises pigs."

12. **Why is sirloin steak not kosher?**

The hindquarters of an otherwise kosher animal are unfit for use according to the Bible (Genesis 32:33). Sirloin steak comes from the hindquarters of the cow. In order for it to be eaten, the sciatic nerve, together with the other tendons and arteries, must be removed from the slaughtered animal. This precept is a constant reminder of the Divine Providence to Israel, as exemplified in the experience of Jacob, who walked away with a limp after defeating the mysterious "angel" and having his name changed to "Israel."

13. **Why does the Torah have such an aversion to the eating of blood?**

A biblical law addressed to all people, Jews and non-Jews, forbids consuming an animal's blood. (Genesis 9:4 and Leviticus 17:10–14). "The blood is the life," the Bible rules, and therefore the blood of a dead animal is drained from the slaughtered creature and covered with earth. Later, the meat must be salted until all traces of blood are removed.

It is likely that Judaism's abhorrence at the possibility of consuming even a drop of blood is related to the general abhorrence of bloodshed in the Jewish community. Wherever they have lived, Jews have committed fewer crimes of violence and bloodshed than their non-Jewish neighbors. Unless one assumes that Jews are genetically different, this must be because of some different values they practice. Keeping kosher, it seems, has helped civilize the Jewish spirit.

14. **What does the word "pareve" mean on a food product?**

Products such as salt, sugar, and coffee—that is, all nonmeat and nondairy products—are considered neutral, or pareve. Such products generally do not require kosher certification, yet nonetheless food manufacturers under rabbinic supervision often do print the seal of a certifying organization on the package.

❋ Jews and the Community

1. Does Judaism believe in equality of the sexes?

In bygone years societies were patriarchal. With only a few exceptions, men were the political, social, and religious leaders. They enjoyed numerous legal and religious rights denied to women and a distinctly superior social status.

Despite this inequality, however, the position of women in ancient Israel was considerably above that of their sisters in other parts of the world. Because women were so fully occupied with their domestic duties, Jewish law excused (but did not prohibit) them from any rituals that must be performed at a specific time.

Today, in the Conservative, Reconstructionist, and Reform movements, synagogues for the most part are egalitarian, and equal opportunity is extended to men and women. There are women presidents of synagogues, and now even women rabbis and cantors. The Orthodox movement still believes in the separation of the sexes, where men and women sit separately at worship services. To date no Orthodox woman has been ordained as a rabbi or cantor.

2. Do Jews have parochial schools?

Yes, hundreds of thousands of Jewish children are being sent to Jewish day schools. The curriculum of the Jewish all-day school parallels that of the public schools for half a day. The remaining hours of the day are devoted to Judaic studies. The Conservative movement's day schools are called "Solomon Schechter schools," named after the first president of the Jewish Theological Seminary of America in New York. The Reform movement's day schools are affiliated with Pardes.

3. **What is the attitude of Judaism to the elderly?**

Judaism has always placed a premium on the experience that comes with years. In Bible times the elders were the advisers to the leaders of the Jewish community. Reverence for the aged was translated into practical provisions for their care. Already in the Middle Ages, the Jewish community built homes for the elderly. A great rabbinic thinker, the Bratzlaver Rebbe, once said that "the prosperity of any country is directly related to its treatment of the aged."

4. **Is there a Jewish attitude toward censorship?**

There is no word for "censorship" in classical Hebrew and little precedent for its practice in ancient Jewish tradition. In medieval times the atmosphere of censorship that permeated the Western world did not leave Judaism untouched. Some religious leaders denounced the reading of books that raised doubts in the minds of the faithful. A few overzealous rabbis forbade their followers to study the liberal writings of Moses Maimonides. In the seventeenth century, the philosopher Baruch Spinoza, a religious radical, suffered the blow of intolerance from his own religious brethren.

In more recent times we have returned to the Jewish tradition that censorship of any kind is not a constructive force in character development. Sound moral character grows out of learning to choose from the open marketplace of human thought those concepts which are creative and worthwhile.

5. **Why do Jews often concern themselves with the rights of other minority groups?**

Jews have often been the victims of tyranny and oppression. It is a primary tenet of Judaism to fight against the mistreatment of any human being, no matter what race or nationality. Sympathy for the misfortunes of their fellow human beings has become a part of the Jewish way of life. Kindness to strangers is a constant theme in the Five Books of Moses.

6. **Why do Jews have a reputation for being smart?**

There is no biological or statistical evidence that Jews are smarter than anyone else. So this reputation is probably a result of the emphasis that Judaism places on education. Giving their children an education is considered one of the most important religious obligations of Jewish parents. The ideal education is achieved when both home and school prepare children to take their place in the world. The importance placed on the value of an education has continued to the present time, and Jewish parents continue to look to send their children to the finest schools and encourage them to attain a college education. Consequently, many Jews in our country continue to be high achievers, and, although a minority, Jews have produced an extraordinarily large number of Nobel Prize winners in many subject areas.

7. Why are Jews often associated with politically liberal causes?

Although the majority of Jews in the United States have gone from being poor twentieth-century immigrants to successful, integrated members of American society, they have remained overwhelmingly liberal in their politics. Known for usually voting Democratic, Jews make up the one ethnic group the majority of whom consistently vote against their own personal economic interests. On social issues, too, the Jewish community has generally stood behind liberal causes.

8. Why have so many people hated Jews throughout history?

Throughout history, antisemitism has been directed against Judaism and its values. It is caused by a variety of socioeconomic and cultural factors. One theory is that Jews were hated in the medieval world because they were moneylenders. For centuries, the papacy and other powerful Christian institutions maintained that Jews were evil because they had killed Christ. Some attribute antisemitism to the Jews' being defiantly different from the majority society, isolated and keeping to themselves. Others have attributed hatred for Jews to the perception, largely mythical, that they are very wealthy.

9. Is it possible to be excommunicated in Judaism?

In the Middle Ages, Jewish communities were granted considerable autonomy, and rabbis had the authority to deal with civil and religious transgressions. Rabbinical courts were established, and excommunication, or banishment from the social and religious life of the community, was meted out as a severe punishment.

During the past century, a ban of excommunication has rarely been issued in Jewish life. Today the ban might be seen in traditional Orthodox communities when a man refuses to give his wife a divorce. In Israel, religious courts are empowered to imprison a recalcitrant husband who refuses to give his wife a religious divorce, although women's groups complain that the courts rarely exercise their power.

❋ Medical Ethics

1. **What does Judaism have to say about abortion?**

If you ask a rabbi about the Jewish view of abortion, the answer is almost always the same: "Tell me the case."

There are two extreme viewpoints in the abortion controversy. One says there is no moral justification for abortion. The other proclaims that it is a woman's right to have an abortion on demand. The debate continues to be a heated one.

These days, there are many rabbinic opinions on the subject of abortion. Because Judaism believes that life is a gift from God, and is sacred, rabbinic writings point to a restriction of the legitimacy of abortion to a narrow range of cases. Jewish law requires abortion when the woman's life or health—physical or mental—is threatened by the pregnancy. Jewish law permits abortion when the risk to the woman's life or health is greater than that of normal pregnancy but not so great as to constitute a clear and present danger to her.

2. **What is Judaism's attitude toward assisted suicide?**

Life is a gift from God, and God alone has the right to make decisions about life and death. Therefore, suicide is morally wrong. Since suicide itself is prohibited, aiding a suicide is also forbidden according to Jewish law.

3. **Does Jewish law permit stem cell research?**

There is no single view that can answer whether Jewish law permits stem cell research. There are, however, many different opinions on the subject. Reform rabbis posit that an isolated fertilized egg does not enjoy the full status of personhood. Therefore they support stem cell research, on the basis of the primary responsibility to save human life, a supreme Jewish value.

4. **What does Jewish law say regarding organ transplants?**

Today most rabbinic authorities in all branches of Judaism would permit the donation of one's organs to benefit another. Two main issues work in tandem with the issue of organ donation. Saving a person's life and acting kindly toward others are values so sacred in Judaism that if a person's organ can be used to preserve someone else's life, using the organ in that way is actually an honor to the deceased.

The greatest consensus of rabbinic opinion holds that eye or corneal transplants are permissible. Transplantation of a healthy kidney to replace a patient's nonfunctioning kidney is also permissible. The general rule is that the rabbis permit organ transplants when they can be accomplished without major risk to the donor's life or health.

The most restrictive rabbinic opinion would permit donations only when there is a specific patient who stands to lose his or her life or an entire physical faculty. According to this opinion, for example, if the patient can see out of one eye, a cornea may not be removed from a dead person to restore vision to the other eye. Only if both eyes are failing, so that the potential recipient would lose all vision and therefore incur serious danger to life and limb, may a transplant be performed.

Each year in November there is a National Donor Sabbath. Clergy in all denominations speak to their members to try to raise awareness about the critical need for organ and tissue donors and discuss their religious beliefs and traditions related to this topic.

5. According to Judaism, when is it permissible to declare someone officially dead?

Today the generally accepted rabbinic opinion is that a flat electroencephalogram, indicating cessation of spontaneous brain activity, is sufficient to determine a person's death.

6. Would Judaism allow for the selling of one's organs and body parts for profit?

Judaism would not permit people to sell their body parts for profit. The Jewish belief is that God owns everything, including our bodies. Our bodies are considered on loan to us from God, to be returned to God at the time of death. The immediate implication of this belief is that Jews do not have the right to sell that which does not belong to them.

7. Do Jews believe in the use of birth control?

In Jewish law, it is the male who is legally responsible for propagation. This argues against use of a condom, at least until he has fulfilled that duty. Nevertheless, many rabbinic authorities posit that condoms may be used if unprotected sexual intercourse poses a medical risk to either spouse, for condoms do offer some measure of protection against disease, and the duty to maintain health and life supersedes the positive duty of the male to propagate.

From the point of view of Jewish law, the diaphragm is the most favored form of contraception, for it prevents conception and has little, if any, impact on the woman's health. If the contraceptive pill or implant is not contraindicated by a woman's age or body chemistry, it is usually the next most favored in Judaism.

8. **What does Judaism say about homosexuality?**

There are a variety of Jewish views on homosexuality. Homosexual conduct between males is mentioned much more frequently and more heavily condemned in the traditional Jewish sources than such conduct between females. New medical knowledge about the origin of homosexuality has led some branches of Judaism to rethink their stance against homosexuality, in some cases to the point of equating monogamous and loving homosexual relations with the same type of heterosexual relations.

9. **What is the Jewish view on euthanasia?**

Jewish law strictly forbids any attempt to cut short the life of a dying person. Any direct act which brings death nearer is forbidden, even if the person to whom it is done will die soon in any event. Today it is generally held that a sufferer in agony can be given injections of pain-killing drugs even though these may have the eventual effect of cutting life short. It is also generally agreed that doctors are not obliged to resort to artificial means of keeping an incurable and greatly suffering patient alive if without these means nature will take its course and the patient will die.

❋ Jews and Christians

1. Do Jews believe that Judaism is the only true religion?

There are different ways of answering this question. Those who believe literally in the supernatural revelation of the Torah might say that Judaism is the only true religion but would add that other religions are also true to the extent that they approximate Judaism. No Jew would say that all religions except Judaism alone are false.

Many Jews, on the other hand, take the position that no religion has the whole truth, and therefore it is misleading to speak of one true religion. They think of religious truth as discovery rather than revelation and believe that all religions have discovered some truth. They add that the Jewish people has a special genius for religious discovery and, therefore, Judaism is the best religion.

Others maintain that it is absurd to talk of best and better religions, since religious truth cannot be measured or compared. All religions are different. And differences need no defense.

2. What do Jews believe about Christianity?

The Jewish tradition includes the following ideas about Christianity:

1. Christians believe, in common with Jews, that the Bible is of divine origin and was given through Moses. Their interpretations of the Bible, however, frequently differ. As a daughter-religion of Judaism, Christianity shares with us the great spiritual enterprise of making known the glory of God for the salvation of humanity.

2. Christianity is spreading the worship of God and the knowledge of Bible to places and people that have not come in contact with these blessings. Through Christianity, the Torah, the law of God, is reaching people everywhere.

3. For non-Jews, Christianity is a monotheistic and true religion. The Christian belief in the Trinity, however, clouds the clarity of the concept of God's oneness, and therefore Jews do not regard the Trinity as an acceptable way of understanding God.

4. Christianity has many admirable traits and righteous principles. These are all to be found in Judaism.

5. The morals of Christianity are the morals of Judaism. The great commandments of Christianity—"you shall love God with all your heart and soul and might," and "you shall love your neighbor as yourself"—are taken verbatim from the text and spirit of Judaism.

6. Christianity is not the fulfillment of Judaism. Rather, it is the acceptance of much of Judaism, the adaptation of part of it, and the adoption of other elements alien to it. It is a unique development of an offshoot of Judaism.

3. **Why did Christianity change from a Jewish sect to a separate religion?**

At the beginning of the first century of the common era, there was no difference between Judaism and Christianity. Christians were one of several Jewish sects, and their teachings either paralleled, paraphrased, or quoted verbatim beliefs current among the Jews of the time. Jesus's Sermon on the Mount was a Jewish sermon.

Christianity could have remained a Jewish sect. It was Paul, a pious traditional Jew, who brought about the separation of Christianity from Judaism. In his ambition to win over the vast non-Jewish population of the Roman Empire, he created an independent Christian Church. Almost everything Paul taught had some basis in Jewish tradition.

In the course of time, Christianity absorbed and assimilated some of the ideas and practices of the ancient world's non-Jewish cultures. Doctrines such as the virgin birth, the mystery of a dying God, the Trinity, and the adoration of saints widened the gap between Judaism and Christianity until a total separation resulted.

4. **What are some common elements of Judaism and Christianity?**

Elements in common include the principles that there is one God, that Jewish scripture is sacred, that there is a Messiah, that every human being has a soul which is immortal, and that God can be reached by prayer. Differences include the Christian beliefs in the Trinity and the divinity of Jesus, the concept of original sin, and the sacraments. Christianity considers the New Testament to be an additional revelation, and Christians believe that man's ultimate purpose is to enter the Kingdom of God in heaven.

5. **Is it true that Jews shouldn't go to church?**

Many Jews have attended churches with Christian friends and neighbors, both for regular Sunday services and for special ceremonies such as confirmation or a

funeral. They go to church, however, as visitors, not participants. Therefore it would be inappropriate to expect a
Jew to kneel during services, since kneeling is antithetical
to the Jewish tradition. Each year my synagogue has an
ecumenical Thanksgiving service with a Methodist church,
meeting every other year in the church. The service consists of readings and prayers that Judaism and
Christianity have in common, and the tradition has now
been going on for more than two decades.

6. **Do Jews accept converts?**

Yes. Jews have always accepted converts and always
will. Throughout the ages, many non-Jews have been
attracted by the reasonableness of the Jewish religion and
have chosen to become Jews by choice. It is said that more
than ten thousand non-Jews convert to Judaism each year
in America.

7. **What is the Jewish attitude toward Christians?**

The Jewish attitude toward non-Jews is set forth in the
biblical injunctions "you shall love your neighbor as yourself" and "love the stranger." A Christian is more than a
neighbor and a stranger to the Jew. A Christian is a brother who worships the same God. Love is the only word we
have to express the attitude of the Jew toward the
Christian.

8. **Why does Judaism reject the doctrine of original sin?**

St. Augustine was the first theologian to teach that
man is born into this world in a state of sin. Christians
believe that it is only through the acceptance of Jesus that

the grace of God can return to man so that he can be saved. Jews believe that we enter the world free of sin, with a soul that is pure and untainted.

9. **Can a Jew be a member of a church choir?**

Since the hymns sung by a church choir often contain references to the Trinity and to Jesus, views that are antithetical to Jewish belief, rabbis of all denominations have expressed disapproval of Jews who join church choirs and sing hymns that articulate religious concepts contrary to the spirit of Jewish belief.

10. **Can a non-Jew become a member of a synagogue?**

In Jewish law, one can carry out Jewish religious obligations only if one is in fact a Jew. A non-Jew is not expected, or permitted, to recite blessings over the Torah, because the commandments do not apply to non-Jews. For this reason, a non-Jew is not accepted as a member of a synagogue even if married to a Jew. It should be noted that there is generally no objection to a non-Jewish spouse attending worship services or joining in social activities or attending adult classes in a synagogue. There are some Reform synagogues that grant membership to persons not of the Jewish faith.

11. **What is the Jewish attitude toward Christmas?**

As a religious celebration in commemoration of the birth of Jesus, Christmas has no significance whatsoever for Jews, since the most basic point of difference between Judaism and Christianity lies in the Christian belief in the divinity of Jesus.

✳ Jewish Denominations

1. What is the difference between Reform and Conservative Judaism?

Reform Judaism is more liberal than Conservative Judaism, and allows for more personal autonomy. Conservative Judaism adheres to rabbinic law and the later law codes and is much slower in making changes. Thus, for example, Conservative Judaism stands for keeping the dietary laws, whereas in Reform Judaism one is not required to keep kosher. Reform Jews deny a belief in resurrection of the dead, even omitting traditional references to it in their prayerbooks, but Conservative Judaism continues to adhere to belief in an afterlife.

Reform Jews have eliminated references to a human Messiah from their prayerbook. Conservative Judaism still believes in the possibility of the coming of a human Messiah.

Conservative rabbis do not perform interfaith marriages between a Jew and a Christian, but some Reform rabbis will perform such a ceremony.

2. Which group is largest: Reform, Conservative, or Orthodox?

The Orthodox movement is the smallest of the three major branches in the United States but claims the lion's share of synagogues. Of the 3,727 synagogues in the

150

United States, 40 percent are Orthodox, 26 percent Reform, and 23 percent Conservative. Many of the Orthodox synagogues are small, with fewer than fifty families, compared to Reform and Conservative synagogues that often have hundreds of families.

3. **Who are the Hasidim?**

Hasidism, the religious movement of the Hasidim, arose in the eighteenth century in Europe. Its founder, Rabbi Israel, revealed himself in the early 1700s as a healer and leader. He was known as the "Master of the Good Name." One of his fondest teachings was that God desires the heart, which is interpreted to mean that God prefers a pure religious spirit to knowledge of rabbinic law.

The best-known group of Hasidim in the United States are the Lubavitcher, headquartered in Brooklyn. Hasidic dress for men generally consists of a white shirt, and a long black frock coat with a black hat, sometimes with fur adorning it. This replicates the dress of East European Jews in the sixteenth century. Hasidic women wear long-sleeved dresses that extend down past their ankles as a sign of modesty and humility. Hasidic men do not shave their sideburns, and therefore they have long sideburns which are often curled to keep them looking more attractive.

4. **What is Reconstructionist Judaism?**

The youngest of the religious movements in American Judaism is Reconstructionism. It is a uniquely American movement because it began in the United States, unlike the other religious groups that began in Europe and were transplanted to America. The Reconstructionist movement began in 1922, and its leaders and thinkers are all

Americans. Reconstructionism is based on the work of Rabbi Mordecai Kaplan, who founded a synagogue in the early 1920s called the Society for the Advancement of Judaism. This became the laboratory for developing his ideas about reconstructing Judaism.

The most important of the Reconstructionist teachings is that Judaism is a changing, evolving, developing civilization. Judaism is more than just worshiping God and performing commandments and saying prayers. Judaism is a civilization, and the Jewish people have created their own art, music, language, folkways, and customs.

5. Is there such a thing as a black Jew?

When I was a student in rabbinical school, I used to visit the black synagogue in Harlem. Rabbi Wentworth Arthur Matthew, born in the West Indies, was the rabbi, and he trained many rabbis who later founded synagogues in various places in the United States and the Caribbean.

The emergence of Judaism among people of African descent in the first half of the twentieth century is said to have been made possible by a combination of factors. One was a strong religious tradition in the background of those who became Jewish, embodying Jewish practices from an early but unclear source.

The possible origins of these Hebraic traditions could be traced to West Africa, where a number of tribes have customs so similar to Judaism that an ancient connection or maybe even descent from one of the Ten Lost tribes is conjectured. Another possibility for these well-documented practices is association with Jewish slave owners and merchants in the Caribbean and North America.

According to the *Jewish Encyclopedia*, no reliable statistics exist for the number of black Jewish congregations or for total membership, but estimates suggest a few dozen distinct groupings in cities such as New York, Chicago, Philadelphia, Boston, and Cincinnati, with membership between two thousand and six thousand.

✳ Israel

1. Why is Jerusalem so holy for the Israelis and the Jews?

In 1000 B.C.E. King David made Jerusalem the political and religious center of Israel. It is the city where the holy Temple was built, and where some of the major Jewish prophets uttered their thoughts. Throughout the centuries of their dispersion, Jews prayed for the return to Zion, the biblical synonym for Jerusalem. Synagogues, wherever in the world they were built, were oriented toward Jerusalem (and the practice is followed to this day). Jewish prayers contain numerous references to Jerusalem, and Jews pray everyday for its welfare. Jerusalem, of course, was the scene of Jesus's last ministry and his crucifixion as well. Moslems, too, consider Jerusalem holy, believing it to be the site from which Mohammed ascended to heaven.

2. What exactly is Zionism?

Zionism is both a religious and a political movement. As part of their faith, Jews pray (some of them three times daily) asking God to rebuild Zion. Jerusalem is part of the Jewish marriage ceremony, the Passover Seder, and even the mourning ritual.

Politically, Zionism is a movement to re-establish Jews as a people in the land of Israel. A Zionist believes that such a homeland will help to secure the welfare of Jews throughout the world. The official Zionist movement was formally organized in 1897. Theodor Herzl is considered to have been its founder. Although the movement's followers were united in general purpose, they differed in their specific interests. Some felt that Palestine would be a refuge for the oppressed, others hoped it would bring a rebirth of Jewish culture. Today there are many Zionist movements throughout the world. Some of the more famous ones are Hadassah, the Jewish women's organization, and various American Zionist youth groups.

3. **Why does Israel welcome so many immigrants?**

Israel's policy of free immigration is a reflection of a people moved to compassion for their suffering brothers and sisters. Israel has received thousands and hundreds of thousands of immigrants for all over the world. Especially to be noted are the Jews from Ethiopia and the Soviet Union. Israeli citizens believe that every Jew who wants to settle in Israel has an inalienable, God-given right to do so.

4. **Are Israeli Jews more religious than those in the United States?**

A large majority of Israelis are not traditional. There are, to be sure, Conservative, Reform, Reconstructionist, and Orthodox synagogues throughout Israel. The pattern of religious observance in Israel varies little from that of other lands.

5. **Is the State of Israel controlled by a religious authority?**

Although Israel has two Chief Rabbis (one Ashkenazic and the other Sephardic), the State of Israel is not governed by the rabbinate. The Israeli government is democratically elected by all of the country's citizens (including non-Jews) and represents their political will. The laws of Israel are civil laws, except those that govern marriage and the family. There is no religious test for public office—a prime minister or a cabinet minister need not be a synagogue-goer. Several members of parliament are Arabs.

The Israeli Parliament has 120 members. In American terms, it can be best understood as a combination of the Senate and the House of Representatives, and a body in which the head of state and the cabinet sit as well. In Israeli elections, voters select parties. If a party gets 20 percent of the votes, then it is entitled to 20 percent of the seats in the Parliament. It is the party, therefore, not the voters, that determines who will sit in Parliament. The Israeli voting system encourages a much larger number of parties than the system in the United States, since a party need capture only about 1 percent of the popular vote to earn a seat in Parliament.

6. **What exactly is a kibbutz?**

The kibbutz movement started as farm colonies run on a share-and-share-alike basis. All the members of a kibbutz shared equally in the work according to their individual talents and capacities. Kibbutz life existed before there was a State of Israel. After the State of Israel was established in 1948, the agricultural cooperatives declined in importance. There are still kibbutzim in Israel. Some of the more wealthy ones have tourism as their major attraction.

Another interesting kind of farm settlement is called a moshav. It differs from a kibbutz in that people own their own homes, live full-time with their families, and dispose of their income as they wish.

7. **Is an American Jew's first loyalty to Israel or to America?**

An American Jew ought to be supportive of the State of Israel and concerned for its welfare, but his or her first loyalty would be to the United States.

8. **Why do Israelis have a reputation for being harsh?**

Because Israel is surrounded by many enemy countries, its people must always be alert and on the lookout for potential danger. Most Israeli boys and girls are drafted into army duty immediately following high school, and they continue to serve as reservists until their mid-fifties. I suppose that the mind-set of an Israeli who must always be on the lookout for danger would likely lead to being more tense, and even more aggressive.

9. **Why is Israel often called the Holy Land?**

Because Israel was the home of the Hebrew Bible and the prophets, it has come to be known as the Holy Land both for Jews and Christians. And the language of Israelis, Hebrew, is known as the Holy Tongue because it was the language in which God gave Moses the Torah (the first five books of the Bible).

10. **What is Israel's national anthem?**

It is called Hatikvah (meaning "The Hope"), and it was written by a Hebrew poet whose name was Naphtali Hertz Imber. The poem's recurring stanza expresses the Jewish people's enduring desire to return to Zion:

Our hope is not yet lost

The hope of two thousand years
To be a free people in our own land
The land of Zion and Jerusalem.

11. **Why does Israel's army have such a good reputation?**

Man for man, the Israeli army, known by its Hebrew initials as Tzahal (from *Tzvah Haganah LeYisrael*, meaning "Israel Defense Forces"), and in English as the IDF, is generally regarded as one of the best in the world. Its name describes the army's self-image. It is intended to fight only in defense of the Jewish people and the country.

The IDF's fighting reputation was established in 1948 during the so-called War of Independence. At that time, six Arab armies simultaneously invaded Israel. Though vastly outnumbered, the Israelis succeeded in overcoming the enemy.

Unlike the armies of surrounding Arab countries, the IDF is largely based on its reserve forces. Only some 140,000 men and women are on active duty at any one time. Within forty-eight hours, the IDF can complete its reserve call-up and become an army of over 600,000.

12. **Why is the Western Wall so sacred to Jews?**

When Rome destroyed the second Jerusalem Temple in 70 C.E., only one outer wall remained standing. This remnant of the Temple became the holiest spot in the world for Jews. The praying at the Wall was so heartfelt that non-Jews began calling it the "Wailing Wall."

From 1948 until 1967 the Wall was under Jordanian rule. In 1967, after the Six-Day War, the Wall was liberated and Jews returned to praying there. Today, the custom of inserting written prayers into the Wall's tiny cracks and crevices is so widespread that some American-Jewish newspapers carry advertisements for services that insert such prayers on behalf of the sick.

13. **What is the Law of Return?**

The first law passed by the Israeli Parliament after Israel's establishment as a state was the Law of Return, which guarantees all Jews the right to immigrate to Israel and claim immediate citizenship. It is probably the most important piece of legislation ever passed by the Parliament. Interestingly, when a Jew immigrates to Israel, it is called the act of making *aliyah* (meaning "to ascend"). An Israeli who emigrates from Israel is called a *yored* ("one who goes down"). The term accurately describes the general contempt Israeli society has for a Jew who leaves the country to reside elsewhere.